D0371281

THE
IN-CREDIBILITY
FACTOR

To my wonderful Anty Pauline,

With love and best wishes,

Teresa oo

OXOX

30 **Stories and Strategies Every Entrepreneur Needs to Know**

TERESA KRUZE
AND TERRY BEECH

The In-Credibility Factor

Copyright 2014 by Teresa Kruze and Terry Beech

Book Jacket by Joni McPherson
Book designed by Janet Rouss

ISBN # 978-0-9879507-0-3

First Paperback Edition.

Dedications

To my Mom and Dad who taught me I could do anything, to my sister who loved me through everything, and my husband, Gary, who said he could hardly wait to see what I was going to do next.

Now that's something.

Teresa Kruze

To my wife, Ravi, and my brother, Doug.

Terry Beech

Acknowledgements ✳

I would often read through an author's acknowledgements page and marvel at all the people they wanted to thank. I wondered, "Did it really take that many people to inspire, write, and craft a book?" Yes, indeed it does.

My heart is so full of gratitude as I look at all we've accomplished and I want to personally acknowledge the people who have contributed greatly to the book you are holding in your hands right now.

To all the wonderful entrepreneurs who took time from their busy schedules to talk to me, thank you for sharing your stories and speaking from your heart. Not every pathway to success is paved with gold, so I commend you for being so honest about your journeys and allowing me to tell the real story so all of us can learn from one another.

To the incomparable Terry Beech, thank you for linking arms with me and believing in this project as much as I do. Inspiration + Tools = Success for the reader and *The In-Credibility Factor* is much stronger with your contribution.

To my editor, Sue Bennett, thank you for your knowledge, expertise, and gentle guidance. You never lost faith in me and your honesty and belief in my abilities powered me on to the finish line. To my friend and colleague, John Ignatowicz, thank you for your assistance in the early stages of editing this book and for giving me the help I needed to proceed.

I've never known a creative muse before but I found the best in Janet Rouss. I can't thank you enough for coming in at the eleventh hour to design and format the book. You are an award winning package of design, creativity, and branding, plus you are an amazing friend. Joni McPherson, you are a designer extraordinaire and I am so grateful your beautiful cover graces the front and back of the book.

I'd also like to send a big tip of the hat to two women who have no idea how much their contribution and support have meant to me. To Colleen McMorrow, you have helped put *The In-Credibility Factor* on the map and one day you'll understand just how large your contribution to the success of this book has been. Charlotte Empey, you are a treasure, a mentor, and someone whose impact on my life and career has been immeasurable. As Editor-in-Chief at Metro News, you took me under your wing and gave me an opportunity to become a columnist for your paper. Your vision and belief in my abilities set *The In-Credibility Factor* in motion, and for that I will be forever grateful.

Finally, I need to thank my husband and partner, Gary. You have given me an amazing gift. You encouraged me to go after what I wanted in life and have stood beside me through so many transitions, heartbreaks, and defining moments. Now it's time to celebrate.

I send hugs of gratitude to you all. Now let's get reading and become inspired!

Teresa Kruze

Contents

30 Inspiring Entrepreneurial Stories

🔟 Tools and Strategies Every Entrepreneur Needs to Know

Introduction _____

"The best is yet to come."

I stood in the lobby of CityTV in Toronto staring at the small bronze plaque underneath the picture of cable, wireless, and media mogul, Ted Rogers. I had always been a fan of the maverick entrepreneur and his famous quote, "Never, ever give up." Now there was a new bit of wisdom for me to ponder. Ted Rogers had nerves of steel and pursued life and business with the tenacity of a bulldog. Even now, after he had earned his boardroom chair in heaven, Rogers was still inspiring people on earth, telling us to be strong and to look forward to the future. "The best is yet to come." It was advice I placed in my heart.

I believe it doesn't matter where we are in life, what age, gender, culture, or ethnicity, we have the capacity to change our destiny and create the future the way we want it to unfold. When I left TSN after fourteen years as a sportscaster, everyone thought I was crazy. I always had one response, "Never sit in the rocking chair of life and say, I wish I would have." With the love of a very supportive husband, I set out on my journey of challenge and change, hosting television talk shows, becoming a news anchor, singing in a R&B band, and writing a national column on entrepreneurs for Metro News. Many people kept encouraging me to write a book about what I had learned and after several years of thought and careful planning, *The In-Credibility Factor* was born.

This book is a collection of some of the best minds in business today. They all come from humble beginnings and have gone on to enjoy life-changing success. You will read about billionaires, millionaires, small business owners, and people who have started companies in their home. They all have a story to tell, and when I approached them about sharing and inspiring a new generation of entrepreneurs, not one of them hesitated. I encourage you to read their stories of success, failure, transformation, and perseverance and at the end of every chapter you will find five bullet points of success. While conducting the interviews, I asked each person to imagine an aspiring entrepreneur sitting in their office (that's you, dear reader) and to tell them five of the most important points they need to know when starting and running a successful business. Many of the points appear to be common sense, however, when you put them together and realize what they have done with a few simple, core beliefs, you will find their points of advice turn into entrepreneurial magic.

Along with the thirty inspiring stories, you will find thirty tools, tips, and strategies from award winning entrepreneur, Terry Beech. I approached the successful businessman and adjunct professor about contributing to this book so it would become a complete package of information to get you started on your entrepreneurial journey. He has done an amazing job and his chapters are an informative powerhouse of thought-provoking inspiration and practical advice.

Now it's in your hands. Read this book, believe in your vision, be creative, persevere, and, as Ted Rogers said, "Never, ever give up because… the best **is** yet to come."

Teresa

Inspiring Entrepreneurial Stories

Teresa Kruze

You Gotta Wanna

Jim Pattison
Chairman and Chief Executive Officer
The Jim Pattison Group

He is a superstar business magnate and, according to Forbes, is worth 5.5 billion dollars. Jim Pattison has come a long way from growing up in poverty and watching his family struggle to make ends meet. He bought a car dealership in Vancouver, started a leasing company, and then moved into media, the food industry, and other ventures. Today, The Jim Pattison Group is Canada's third largest privately owned company, but when I ask him to share his story he quickly stops me.

"At our company, we don't talk about ourselves," he says quietly. "We're not fancy, and we didn't do much different. We just worked hard."

After much cajoling, I finally convince him to talk about business, and the affable but tough billionaire is willing to share his thoughts on being an entrepreneur.

"When there's lots of change in the world there's also lots of opportunity. You have to follow up on the opportunities. If you stick with what you believe in, you'll be successful, but it's all about hard work and timing."

To understand the impact Jim Pattison has made in the corporate world, you have to know more about his history, his values, and what drives him as a businessman.

Jim's solid work ethic came from his parents, Chandos 'Pat' Pattison and mom, Julia. Growing up as an only child on the prairies during the Great Depression, life was tough in Luseland, Saskatchewan. Jim was only three years old when his dad let him hold the steering wheel of the family car. That experience left a lasting impression on the young boy because he fell in love with the automobile.

In 1935, Pat moved his family to Vancouver and got a job selling cars. On weekends, when all the other children were out playing with their friends, Jimmy was at the dealership shining the impressive looking autos in the showroom and learning the skills of the sales trade by listening to his dad.

A fast learner, there was no question that selling was in little Jimmy's blood. When he was seven, he peddled garden seeds door-to-door, then graduated to pots and pans. Years later, in a CBC television interview, he explained how he could improve his odds of getting in the door and making a sale.

"I learned that if I whistled going up the stairs, my odds of getting into the house went up. Some wouldn't even answer the door, but if you were whistling, people were interested in happy people and my presentations went up by so much a day."

When he wasn't selling, Jim delivered newspapers and groceries. He was a pageboy at a downtown hotel, working five shifts a week after school and all day Saturday. As industrious and busy as he was, Mom and Dad made sure his life was grounded with regular church services and music. Jim played the trumpet and organ, performing regularly at school, church, and on the street three nights a week for Pentecostal Mission meetings.

When it came time for university, Pat had dreams of his son becoming a lawyer, but Jim enrolled in Commerce at UBC because it was the world of business that fascinated him. That summer, he went looking for a job and applied at used car lots.

"You're too short and too young," he was told over and over again. Topping out at five foot six inches, Pattison isn't a big man but what he lacked in height was made up in talent and hard work. Finally securing a job washing cars for twenty-five dollars a week, and filling in for the salesman on breaks, Jim sold three of the seven cars they had on the lot. He was able to put his wash rag down for good when the manager wisely reconsidered and offered him a fulltime sales job.

When Jim wasn't at the dealership, he was selling cars on the side. One morning, after buying a used car he found in the classified ads, he drove it to school and sold it to a student. Riding the bus back home that night with a fifty dollar profit in his pocket, he was already envisioning his next deal.

Pattison left university in 1950, nine credits short of his degree. By now, Jim was married to his childhood sweetheart, Mary, and with a family on the way he needed a full-time job. His dream was to own a used car company but, unable to buy the lot he wanted, he managed a new dealership for Dan McLean. Jim was tough but fair at Bow Mac (Bowell McLean Motor Company) and his strength was closing the deal. He knew how to get his sales team's attention and wasn't afraid to fire an employee with the lowest monthly sales.

Pattison picked up a card with the words *You gotta wanna* printed on it and says the quote had a huge impact on his life and the way he approached business. It fit in with his core belief that *wanting* to succeed is the most important quality a person can bring to business. Looking back on those dealership days in his 1987 autobiography titled *Jimmy*, Pattison writes, "I realized that no matter how smart a salesman is, how good a family man, how hard working - if he doesn't have the overwhelming desire to achieve, he won't be a good salesman."

By 1961, Pattison was ready to go into business for himself and decided nothing was getting in his way. Convincing a local bank manager to lend him the money, he bought his first Pontiac Buick dealership, telling Mary he was going to be a millionaire before turning forty. Without breaking stride, he began diversifying and acquired radio station CJOR, but it was the takeover of an electrical sign company called Neon Products that launched Pattison into the world of big business.

In 1964, Jim learned about a group called the Young President's Organization. It began in 1950 as a peer network of executives who wanted to become better leaders through education, exchanging ideas, and building contacts. It was an exclusive club, and the people in YPO held the key contacts for what Pattison was looking to build: a Canadian conglomerate. At this point, Pattison had a car dealership, a leasing company, the radio station, and a Muzak franchise. He had a net worth of $760,000 which was a good base, but Jim had something more: persistence and determination.

The takeover of Neon Products was a complicated acquisition involving New York financiers, lines of credit, stock buying, loans being called in, and the inner workings of big business contacts, but Pattison finally closed the deal in 1967. At the age of thirty-nine, he had made good on his promise to Mary; he was a millionaire.

A year later, Pattison acquired supermarket chain Overwaitea Foods, and then set his sights on a bigger prize, Maple Leaf Mills Ltd., one of the biggest food processing and agricultural operations in Canada. Jim pulled out all the stops, but this time the Pattison magic didn't work. The deal collapsed and when the dust settled, Jim was broke, his credibility was shot, and the banks were calling in his personal loans. At the lowest point, he didn't have enough money in the bank for Mary to buy groceries. No one went hungry, but it would take thirteen years for all the lawsuits and counter-suits to be settled.

Financially wounded, Pattison knew his corporation was crippled, but he wasn't sitting around feeling sorry for himself. He started refinancing and restructuring his empire by acquiring more media holdings, a commuter airline, a fish canning operation, and the rights to Orange Crush, which he sold for a forty-four million dollar profit six months later.

Over the years, Pattison has weathered recessions, cutbacks, high interest rates, and numerous governments. He has revamped and retooled his company over and over again, and hasn't been afraid to cut his losses.

"There's no sense in bashing your head against the wall. There are a lot of people with good ideas, but if it's not commercially viable there's no sense sticking with something that isn't going well."

Today, The Jim Pattison Group has sales of more than 7.5 billion dollars and employs 35,000 people. The company holdings are diverse and profitable, comprised of an automotive division, food and beverage, illuminated signs, media, entertainment, real estate, packaging, and periodical distribution. Jim Pattison's vision has become Canada's third largest private company.

He carefully surrounds himself with directors and executives with proven track records and broad experience, such as former B.C. Premier, Glen Clark, who is now company president. Pattison also rewards hard work and loyalty. Maureen Chant, his administrative assistant, has been with the company for fifty years. "It starts with integrity and you have to treat people the way *you* want to be treated," Pattison says firmly from his office in Vancouver.

Now in his ninth decade, Pattison has no plans to slow down or rest. Even in an economy that is slowly recovering from a worldwide recession, he continues to see promise for expansion and growth.

"Don't worry about things you can't control, and know when it's time to move on. You also must be open and willing to change. Remember, it's all about how you treat others."

When he opened his first car dealership in 1961, his mother gave him a poem by James Russell Lowell that Jim keeps framed in his office. It states, "Low aim is crime." Pattison interprets this in his autobiography as, "Failure in life is not the mistakes you make as you attempt things; failure is when you don't try."

"We all make mistakes in business," Jim admits, "but the key is to not *live* with your mistakes."

What's the bottom line from one of the best entrepreneurs ever to emerge from Canada?

"If you work hard and be honest then you'll be successful, and that's about as simple as it gets."

Or, as Jim Pattison believes, "You gotta wanna."

Pattison's Points
✓ Out of adversity and change comes opportunity for something new.
✓ Be alert and keep your eyes open.
✓ Find the resources to make it happen.
✓ Have the best price and quality to be competitive on a world wide basis.
✓ Conduct yourself with integrity.

Everything is an Opportunity

Kelsey Ramsden
President and Founder
Belvedere Place Development, Entrepreneur

Kelsey Ramsden is the owner of a multi-million dollar construction company, the creative force behind a family toy venture, a cancer survivor, and the happily married mother of three young children.

"When I started Belvedere Place Development, all my MBA friends told me I was crazy."

In ten short years, she has proven them wrong. Ramsden has been named the number one female entrepreneur of 2012 by PROFIT and Chatelaine magazines. Who's crazy now?

Ramsden comes from a long line of entrepreneurs. Her father ran a successful international construction firm and her mother started two companies. When six-year-old Kelsey decided she needed money for the candy store, there was only one way to get it. She started a business. Enlisting her three-year-old brother's help, they grabbed two brooms and went outside their Kelowna, B.C. home. The winter snow had recently melted leaving behind a mess of sand, gravel, and leaves in the cul-de-sac. They cleaned the whole street and then barricaded it off. As the residents of the neighbourhood returned home from work they had to pay the young entrepreneur to enter their street.

"I was always coming up with ways to make money," Kelsey tells me, chuckling.

"My parents encouraged our ventures, yet we knew there was a price to pay if we did something wrong."

Free-spirited, resourceful, and very comfortable in the male dominated world of construction, Kelsey's first job was working on the Alaskan Highway when she was fifteen. Standing five feet ten inches tall, the striking blonde made quite the impression as a flag girl.

"It was the best and worst job ever. There was nothing to do and the blackflies bit our ears so much they looked like hamburger. People drove by in their RV's and gave me pop and beer. I sold them to the guys in the camp to make some extra cash."

In 1997, Kelsey's family liquidated everything and moved to the Caribbean to pursue their construction business in a warmer climate. There was a lot of work and money to be made, and Kelsey gained valuable international negotiating skills.

"I worked for my dad, bidding on small jobs, meeting with government officials, and learning how work was being sourced. I also found local connections for the construction supplies we needed."

After three years in the Caribbean, then an adventure trip through India, Kelsey returned to Canada and worked on several construction jobs, including a spillway for a new hydro project. She was building experience and confidence in her chosen profession and was getting ready for the next step. It was time to get a MBA.

Accepted at one of the top schools in the country, Ramsden drove out to London, Ontario, to attend the Richard Ivey School of Business at Western University. Ramsden studied hard and received good marks. She also met an interesting man in her study group.

"He had reddish hair and hockey legs," Kelsey says, laughing. "He was ridiculously smart in a quiet way. I stalked Andrew, to be honest, and after asking him out three times, he finally agreed to go to a party with me."

With her personal life on the upswing, she graduated and began working, only to realize she had made a big mistake with her career.

"You have a lot of debt after getting your MBA so I was brainwashed into becoming a business consultant. I hated it. I was twenty-eight and wanted to start my own construction company. That's when everyone called me crazy, but I had worked in the industry my whole life and knew what I was doing. I got it.

"In 2004, the housing sector was revving up in Kelowna. A land development company asked me to be their project manager. It was four hundred acres of land and the largest development in West Kelowna. I took the job."

Belvedere Place Development was in business.

"We took the land from being zoned agricultural to a master planned community. We subdivided and rezoned the land. I negotiated with another joint venture partner to do all the civil work, putting in the roads, water, and sewer services. It was my first road building job and I managed the development company."

Hiring an accountant full time, Ramsden now had one employee and watched as the company began to grow. Kelsey secured several government contracts and during the summer the payroll swelled to sixty workers, then in the winter it fell back to two.

"Andrew followed me to Kelowna and we were married. Our daughter Sophie was born in 2007, and at this point Belvedere was doing two million a year. We continued growing and the next year we did four million, then eight million. In 2009, we were awarded a ten million dollar job in Fort St. John. Years earlier, I had promised Andrew we would move back to London to be closer to his family and business. I went up to Fort St. John and he took Sophie to London. During the seven months I was on the job, I had three days with my family."

Ramsden knows the meaning of the word sacrifice.

"If you're confident enough in your relationship, you have the capacity to achieve anything. You make phone calls and make it work. You're not going to lose your whole life by choosing your career.

"My son Graeme was born in 2010. Being a newborn, he went with me everywhere while I negotiated through a market that had tanked. He went to the bonding company with me and to the bank when I was asking for a ten million dollar loan. This was my life, and having delivered constantly they didn't care I had a kid on my hip. They were only concerned with how much interest they would make off of me."

Kelsey continued the commute between B.C. and Ontario. She was wearing a lot of hats as a businesswoman, wife, and mother. In 2011, another son, Sam, was born and two months later in January of 2012, her world was rocked to its core.

"I was diagnosed with cervical cancer. I was told it was a deadly, fast-growing kind of cancer and usually people are given eighteen months to live. It doesn't respond to chemotherapy or radiation. The only chance I had was the knife."

Kelsey underwent a radical hysterectomy and despite her powerful, "conquer it all" attitude towards life, there were many times she was overcome with emotion.

"There were several, sitting-on-the-kitchen-floor, rocking moments," she admits. Then I became angry saying, 'Let's kill this cancer.' I called my family and my insurance company. I had recently negotiated a new loan secured by my life insurance. The death rate of my cancer was high and I worried they were going to yank my policy. Thankfully my broker offered me something very expensive and I agreed to it."

Kelsey coaxed her dad out of retirement and convinced her brother, who had recently moved back to Kelowna after selling his business, to help out. Still involved with Belvedere Place Development as President, Ramsden left the daily running of the business to her family while she recuperated from the surgery.

"I had grown my company to a place where my skills and talents had come to a crest. My brother has a different skill-set, so he took over and did a fantastic job. We also needed someone with international experience. My dad stepped in and it was perfect. Now we're exploring ideas in the Caribbean, Africa, and South America. I don't know if we would have expanded as soon as we did had they not come into the business when I became sick. Belvedere did about seventeen million in 2012. Last year we did thirty-five million, doubling our revenue in two years."

The front door suddenly swings open and three excited children come running into the house. Sophie, Graeme, and Sam have come in from day camp and they all want to talk to Kelsey at once. Ramsden stops the interview, takes off her business hat, and slips effortlessly into the role she cherishes, being a mom.

"My kids are home!" she smiles, as her energy level instantly rises to meet their enthusiastic entrance. "Hi bud," she says, leaning down to Graeme who's clutching a picture. "Give me a smooch. Did you make that?" Graeme hands over the artwork to his mom and says Julia gave it to him. "Julia?" Kelsey replies, turning back to me with a smile. "I think my son has an admirer!"

There are hugs and kisses all around and as quickly as the children arrived, they speed off to their rooms. Ramsden returns to business mode, growing thoughtful.

"I have defied the odds," Kelsey continues. "I feel the best thing that happened to me was getting cancer. It put into perspective how amazing moments in life can be with my husband and kids. I have a better grasp on what truly matters and it clarified for me what the best use of my time should be."

Ramsden has expanded her portfolio to other ventures outside of the construction business. Inspired by her growing family, Kelsey created SparkPlay, a digital club for families. Every month, an Adventure Play Pack arrives in the mail. Designed to forge deeper, emotional bonds between parents and their children, the packs focus on play-based learning techniques, building confidence and leadership through high-level problem solving.

"I also have my own website where I blog and do consulting work. I get asked a lot of questions at dinner parties so I'm producing a digital program for people who want to start their own company. I want to be the Oprah of business or Suze Orman on steroids."

Ramsden stresses it's important to be honest with yourself and others about your skill-set. It's okay to admit you don't know it all.

"You have to be honest and open to learning. I go into financial meetings and say, 'I don't understand what you're talking about.' If anyone wants to judge me, that's okay. I'm not going to act until I understand everything so I can make the right deal.

"I feel the key to success in business is all about building good relationships. You must develop an inner confidence. Everyone has middle-of-the-night moments when you're not feeling so sure about yourself or your decisions. You need perseverance balanced with knowing when it's time to throw in the towel. People waste time trying to be right or to prove something. There are times when you have to take it on the chin and say 'You're right, it's not working.'"

Ramsden also believes age should never be a barrier to starting your own business.

"I don't believe it's ever too late. Develop good relationships and find people who are in the industry you want to get into. Learn from them.

"I tell people to come up with an ingenuitive thought about the way you see the world. It's what separates the men from the boys. The mind is the only untapped resource and a playful mentality is key. You have to expose yourself to new challenges and realize everything is an opportunity."

With our business concluded, the multi-millionaire, award-winning entrepreneur moves to the next task on her list. It's the end of the day and it's time to make dinner for her family. Kelsey Ramsden has shown us that with focus, vision, and the right balance in life, some people *can* have it all.

Ramsden's Thoughts on Building a Business

✓ You do not know everything. Seek experience and find mentors willing to work with you.

✓ Do not be afraid to be wrong or fail unless it is life-threatening.

✓ There are people who want "it" as much as you. Work harder than the competition.

✓ Relationships are built, take maintenance, attention and care, then they yield tremendous dividends in business and life. Take time to nurture both.

✓ Your integrity is all you have at the end of the day. Protect it at all costs.

✓ Bonus point: Ponder the word value. What do you value in life? Make a list, put them in order of greatest value, then invest your energy in making them happen.

Game Changing Vision _____

Dr. Alan Ulsifer
CEO and President of FYidoctors

Dr. Alan Ulsifer stared at the simple piece of plastic in his hand, turning it over and examining the fine craftsmanship. Standing at a display at an optical convention in Las Vegas, he knew instantly his life and profession were about to change forever.

"It was called Freeform," Dr. Ulsifer explains, "and they were able to create high quality lenses without a mold. It was a special tool and optically there were huge advantages from a vision standpoint compared to traditional lenses. I thought, 'Wow, this will change everything in the marketplace. How do we start using this technology now?'"

Ulsifer went on to create the largest private optical service company in Canada, change the way people buy vision products and look after their eyes, and was named the EY National Entrepreneur of the Year in 2012. Yet on this day, as he stood in front of the booth, he was blissfully unaware of the long struggle that was in front of him. All he had was the game-changing piece of plastic in his hand, glittering under the convention floor lights. He knew he was on to something big.

Born in North Battleford, Saskatchewan, and moving to Saskatoon when he was four, Alan describes himself as a regular kid who loved to play sports. Ulsifer's entrepreneurial talents emerged early in life when he began buying and selling cars he rebuilt in high school. He worked in a grocery store and later on an oil pipeline, saving money to put himself through school. During university, Alan married his childhood sweetheart, was accepted into the only English-speaking optometry school in Canada, and became a father to his first child when he was still studying to become a doctor. He made the dean's list three times, won numerous awards, and continued playing baseball, basketball, and hockey.

To say Alan Ulsifer achieved a lot in his young life is an understatement.

"After graduation, I moved to Airdrie, Alberta. I wanted to be near a big city but not in it. Calgary was just down the road and Airdrie made sense. I joined a fellow there who had a practice and we opened our second one in Innisfail a year-and-a-half later."

Asked to join the Alberta Optometric Association, Dr. Ulsifer began serving on the regulatory body as a council member.

"It was more political than business and I didn't like it, however, it started me thinking differently. I realized I needed to worry about my patients, what is relevant to them and to not worry about what everyone else is doing."

Looking at his medical practice as more of a business, Alan watched how the industry was evolving. Deciding it was time to change how they practice and market their offices, he began talking to two optometrists in Grand Prairie, Alberta, who were wondering if he'd join forces with them.

"There was a lot of competition in the marketplace and I told them there was an opportunity to do something different. I suggested we create an eye-care centre. The industry was going into more fashion and designer eyeglasses. Optometrist offices only carried traditional eyewear without a big selection. We were seeing people coming to us for eye examinations and going elsewhere for their glasses and contact lenses. I felt we weren't fulfilling the needs of our patients. We had to deal with them as a patient *and* a customer."

It was 1994, and Alan and his partners put together a plan to build a ten thousand square foot eye-care facility with the latest technology. Instead of five hundred frames, they would stock thirty-five hundred and service them in the office laboratory. They would market it aggressively and launch an advertising campaign, an approach which had been previously taboo in their industry. The two optometrists in Grand Prairie bought into the plan, but there was a minor problem.

"I had no money," Ulsifer admits. "I was still recovering from major student debt while becoming a doctor. My partners agreed to put in enough collateral to get it going and the bank lent me my portion. It was a tough pill for my wife to swallow but she believed in me. She had to sign her life away when we secured the funding, so there were several tense moments and challenges."

The shovel hit the ground and they worked with an architect to build a state-of-the-art eye-care facility. They spent hours designing the new building. It was functional, beautiful, and it flowed. Then the project began bleeding red ink.

"We went way over budget. In fact, we came to the point we were so over budget the bank wouldn't give us any more money to finish building. We had to change financial institutions and when we canceled the initial funding I had to pay an eighty thousand dollar penalty."

With financial issues, construction dilemmas and delays, there was a lot of tension building between the four partners. Ulsifer admits opening day of the Northern Vision Centre wasn't extremely happy, however, they moved past their problems quickly when their new eye-care centre proved to be a runaway hit.

"We had amazing success very quickly. It grew dramatically and the whole competitive landscape changed. It became to be the largest volume optometry location in Canada."

With Dr. Ulsifer leading the way, the four partners opened eight satellite offices. Alan was a man on a mission reading books on business and investing in the stock market. They established a real estate company and began accumulating land, homes, commercial property, and apartments.

"Other optometrists heard about our business plan and started visiting Grand Prairie, looking to replicate our practice in other areas. They also were asking for advice which I readily shared. A lot of people had talked about consolidating the industry. There was a little collaboration but no one had taken it too seriously. I was in this category too. I knew it was going to be tough and I wondered what we needed to do to make it work."

While he was pondering the future of his business and what was needed to drive it forward outside of Grand Prairie, it was then that he went to Las Vegas for the convention. As he held the revolutionary eyeglass lens in the palm of his hand, Dr. Ulsifer knew he had found the missing piece to the puzzle.

"In the past," he explains, "optometrists had to buy lenses from the big three manufacturers. It wasn't cheap and they had control of the industry. With Freeform lens technology, optometrists were able to do it themselves. It was a way to vertically integrate."

Alan did the homework and crunched the numbers. Presenting the information to his partners, they knew they weren't big enough to make it economically feasible so he picked up the phone.

"In 2006, I invited ten practices from three provinces to a meeting in Kelowna. Optometrists are notoriously independent but I knew we had to try it. We talked for two days and I told them, 'If we're going to do this, we'll have to come together.'

"We made the pitch and to my surprise all ten said, 'Okay, it sounds good. Let's do it.'"

The group created a committee in 2007 and appointed Dr. Ulsifer chairman. They started having weekly conference calls and meetings to discuss structure. Then the stock market crashed, income trusts disappeared, and the economy was thrown into turmoil.

"It made us question our plan," Ulsifer says, "then we decided it was too good of an idea not to proceed. The challenge was putting together the corporate structure and how it was going to be governed. We had to build the company, and a manufacturing and distribution facility incorporating the new Freeform lens technology. We didn't know how to fund it but we knew we were going to do it."

Dr. Ulsifer and his three partners sold several of their real estate properties and the other groups secured funding. In the eighteen months leading to the launch, they were absorbing a rising amount of costs.

"With the investment in the technology and laboratory construction costs, the money was going and the deals were taking longer. I bled all my personal accounts dry two weeks before we started the company in April of 2008."

FYidoctors launched and immediately ran into numerous problems with the manufacturing facility because the Freeform technology had not been fully developed yet. The quality of lenses was outstanding but there were low yields and it took too long to produce them. Without inventory they were forced to go to outside lens companies to fill their orders.

"I knew our practices were disappointed and I found it very difficult. I drove to every clinic and apologized to the staff for not being able to deliver. I asked for a little more time to get it right. I called it my Tour of Shame."

Alan went into action, changing the management team and operational platform. Months passed, and as the technology improved their delivery issues began to smooth out.

"I never questioned how good an idea the business was, however, I did feel it was vulnerable. It took a year-and-a-half to turn it around but we didn't lose a single clinic. People believed in the concept so much, they dealt with the issues until we were able to fix them."

By 2010, FYidoctors swung into growth mode. Ulsifer began to focus on the company's infrastructure, and expanded their lab and distribution. They created a common medical record and management platform for every practice in the company, something never done before in North America.

From the ten practices that came together in 2006, FYidoctors has grown rapidly to 207 facilities, consisting of 100 franchises and 107 corporate clinics. Not only are they offering Freeform lens distribution, they are offering numerous products along with support systems from marketing and internet strategy, to branding and staff training.

It's been a meteoric rise to the top of the business world and in 2012, Dr. Alan Ulsifer was named the Ernst and Young Entrepreneur of the Year in Canada.

"It's humbling, and the pride in having won has spread throughout the company. It's brought a lot of credibility to FYidoctors and everyone is so happy. We recently had our fifth annual meeting where all the shareholders came together. We achieved something no one had ever done before. It was all based on a story I told them, and the fact that they were still here and we were doing so well was extremely satisfying.

"I don't feel I'm a business expert. A lot of things we've done are common sense. When you're running a good business there is going to be a time to take risks. You have to continue to be innovative but avoid making decisions that have the potential to end the company.

"Before you go into any business, make sure it is relevant to your customer. If it doesn't mean something to them, you're headed for failure. Don't become too emotionally attached to an idea. Make sure you listen to feedback."

Dr. Ulsifer's final words of advice?

"Keep your eyes open for opportunity."

You never know when game-changing vision is going to change your life.

Ulsifer's Ultimate Tips

✓ Work with passionate people.

✓ Work with people smarter than you.

✓ Be a servant leader.

✓ Never assume you fully understand your customer.

✓ Major challenges will occur. Persevere!

Be Daring and Bold

Alexander Levy
CEO and Lead Designer of MyVoice

The little boy reached for a book on the shelf of his elementary school library. As he slowly turned the pages, he had no idea how big an impact the book would have on his life and how it would dramatically affect the lives of hundreds of thousands of people around the world. His big discovery was years down the road, and nine year old Alexander Levy was only concerned about one thing. The book looked exciting and he wanted to read it.

"It was all about robots," Alexander tells me, his voice filled with excitement. "It was beautifully illustrated in full color and it showed robots doing all sorts of tasks from serving tea in Japan to welding a car chassis. It captured my imagination and showed me what people were capable of making." Alex pauses and then says, "You know, it was a huge turning point in my life and one I have never forgotten."

Levy is the CEO and Lead Designer of MyVoice, the developer of innovative, groundbreaking technology changing the way people with speech disabilities communicate with the world. As Alex looks back on his rapid rise, he recalls the other turning points in his life.

"Towards the end of my undergrad while working on my political science degree, I was told I had to get two science credits. I talked my way into a course called Artificial Intelligence and Cognitive Robotics, received top marks, and caught the attention of a professor who told me I should go into the field.

"I made a list of all the robotics competitions in the world and, out of three hundred, I chose one for the U.S. Navy. I only had forty-one days so I put my life savings of eight hundred dollars on the line and recruited a team of people to help me build a robotic boat."

Levy and his team arrived in Norfolk, Virginia, and were immediately shocked at what they encountered. As they looked at the competitors' boats, they realized their $800 creation was in direct competition with models costing $100,000.

"I remember thinking, 'we're so screwed,'" Alex recalls, "but we went ahead anyway. The technical judges from the Navy and the CIA came around and did evaluations. The first day, we won a technical prize and we were beside ourselves. One of the military contractors walked over and said, 'I was talking to my colleagues and we decided if terrorists were to develop an autonomous robotic boat, it would look like yours.'"

Alex and his team looked down at their model constructed out of housing foam and tin roofing. They looked back at the military official.

"He was deadly serious."

The following days were filled with competitions and tasks to see how the robotic boats functioned. When it was over, the team went to the awards ceremony. They had done well, however, Levy knew his creation hadn't outperformed the big, expensive boats.

"We started keeping track of how much prize money was being given out and realized they were holding back. Then an official went to the podium and announced, 'We were completely shocked at how well one team did so we created a special award category.'"

Levy's eight hundred dollar boat and his team of Canadian scientists had impressed the top U.S. military brass so much, they were given the MacGyver Award, named after the popular TV and movie action hero who used science and duct tape to defeat the bad guys. Alex walked to the podium and collected a cheque for one thousand dollars.

"We were the only team to win more prize money than our boat cost to build," Alex says, smiling at the accomplishment. "It was one of the best times of my life. We went home with two hundred dollars and it was great."

Back home in Toronto, Levy went into the fifth year of university. Pursuing a job as a research assistant, he showed the professors his award winning boat and was hired on the spot.

Levy had only been on the job a week when a man walked into the lab and changed the course of his life and career once again. Bill Scott had suffered a stroke seven years previous and it had affected his ability to speak. He had picture flip books and a device similar to the one scientist Stephen Hawking uses where pressing buttons on the screen generates a voice response. Scott had been reading about the new iPhone and was wondering if a communication aid could be made using the latest technology.

Alex was so intrigued he agreed to work on the project in his spare time and set out with two objectives in mind. Using the device's GPS technology, he wanted the aid to be aware of its location so, for example, if it went into a coffee shop, words or phrases would appear making it easier to make a selection. Levy also wanted the ability to customize the phone from another computer, making updates and collaboration easier for the user's family.

"Two weeks later, I had an app. It worked well and Bill was pleased. I took it to Ron Baecker, who is a legendary professor with three degrees from MIT, and has written or edited twenty books and three hundred publications. I was nervous as he looked it over. Professor Baecker put it down and handed me a stack of paper. It was a grant application for the Google Faculty Research Award. A couple of weeks later the craziest thing happened. We took a call from the people at Google asking who they should make the fifty thousand dollar cheque out to."

Alex Levy wasn't even finished university and a huge opportunity had fallen into his lap. "The Federal government matched the grant and it went from just me to a research team conducting studies on kids with autism and adults with strokes. 2010 was a golden year."

Alex and his research team took the new communication device to several conferences. Everyone kept asking him how much the app cost and where it was available for download.

"I was just getting used to my job as a professional researcher and I hadn't counted on becoming a businessperson. I asked several people for advice, thought about it for a few months, and then decided to go for it."

MyVoice was launched on April 6, 2011, and was an immediate hit. Alex was interviewed by all the major TV and radio stations and made the front page of a popular technology site.

"By the end of the first day, we had more than one thousand users. In the previous eighteen months it had only been used by forty or fifty people, so it proved to us the world wanted and needed MyVoice."

Back at the lab the next morning, Alex was called to the phone. It was a young mother who had seen Levy on television the night before and had immediately downloaded the app for her child.

"The mother explained to me her daughter had an Autism Spectrum Disorder and had never been able to speak. She showed her the app and for the first time ever her daughter said, 'I love you.' As I listened to the story I started crying," Alex says honestly. "She was crying. I turned to everyone in the office and told them what had happened. Everyone burst into tears and we were hugging each other. It was an amazing moment because we realized our team had created a product that made a huge difference to a family." Alex grows silent, and then says quietly, "Even now, I still get choked up thinking about it. It was a good day."

Today, MyVoice is used in thirty countries by thousands of people. Since their initial launch, Levy and his team have released thirty new versions of the software serving people with profound disabilities such as blindness, severe tremors, or paralysis. The youngest user of MyVoice is sixteen months old and their oldest is a ninety-six year old man in Germany. They're now helping a wide spectrum of people cope with the effects of Parkinson's, ALS and stroke, accident survivors, and children with cerebral palsy or autism.

Levy admits there have been challenges and he's had to learn how to run a company as he goes along. Simple accounting, project planning, time management, public relations, and licensing have all been a learning process.

"When you incorporate a company, no one hands you a CEO 101 book to make your life easier. I wish I had gone after a commerce degree instead of one in political science," Alex says honestly. "All aspects of business are big deals and you have to learn them all."

Levy says it's important to push yourself as an entrepreneur and to keep momentum going in your favour.

"I tell people to try to take on one ambitious, new project every year. I'm now looking for the next step for MyVoice because I'm very future oriented. I try to steer people away from taking on projects unlikely to have an impact in the world. You meet people who are creating a social network for pets. It's interesting, but you need to ask yourself what the impact and legacy will be."

Levy has only begun his life as an entrepreneur, but already there is an important lesson to be learned from his journey. When life sends you an opportunity, seize it, act quickly, and don't hold back.

"I encourage people to go after an idea that is big, gnarly, and audacious." Levy says. "It's better to fail at doing one audacious thing than to succeed in doing something small."

Alexander's Advice

✓ **Pick your battles.** Strategically and emotionally, it's easier to strive to be the best at one big thing than to be good at many small things. Choose the specific field you want to make a contribution to, and stick with it.

✓ **Think of yourself as an advocate.** The PC revolution wasn't caused by the invention of a new machine; it was caused by the idea that everyone should own a computer. Building an innovative business depends as much on promoting new ideas as it does on promoting new products.

✓ **Describe your mission clearly.** Recruiting others to join your project depends on your ability to inspire them. Nothing works better than being able to clearly describe what you're trying to accomplish, and why it matters.

✓ **Take on bigger, not smaller challenges.** Dwight Eisenhower said, "If a problem cannot be solved, enlarge it." It's surprising, but focusing on seemingly tougher challenges often makes it easier to work quickly, creatively, and effectively.

✓ **Start before you're ready.** Waiting until you feel prepared to take on a new project mostly serves to delay beginning it. Like dancing or cooking, it's better to learn business by doing it right away.

Education is the Key

Greg Roberts
Chairman and CEO
Mary Brown's Famous Chicken and
Taters and P.I. Enterprises Group

Greg Roberts was born in a tiny town on a small island but it never stopped him from dreaming big. Roberts has six companies, over one hundred franchises, two thousand employees, and is expanding internationally. He does most of his business in the fast-food industry and has also diversified into health care, technology, and retail. Not bad for a man who recently turned forty years old.

Triton Island, located off the northeast coast of Newfoundland, is a small, close-knit community of twelve hundred people who rely on the fishing and logging industries to keep them afloat. Roberts wears his heritage proudly and his lilting Newfoundland accent gives him an earthy, unassuming charm. When the conversation turns to business, however, you can tell the heart of a lion beats in his chest.

"I started out working at my father's gas station when I was twelve," Roberts tells me. "I pumped gas and then moved into changing oil and tires. I became used to the retail environment from dealing with customers and understanding what people wanted."

Coming from a smaller centre with geographic challenges never played a role in Greg's development as a business owner. "I'm a sixth generation entrepreneur," he tells me proudly. "Business is what my parents did. They didn't have a big education though and I saw it was stressful. By the time I was in grade seven, I was getting information and videos sent to me from the Canadian Institute of Chartered Accountants."

Lesson One: Learn how to look after your money.

"When I was eighteen I moved to St. John's, Newfoundland, and attended Memorial University where I received a Bachelor of Commerce in Finance. While I was in school I had a bookkeeping service and worked at a gas station."

Greg was employed at a firm in St. John's for the next two and half years while he worked on his Chartered Accountant designation. Learning about the business world and how to tie together academia with practical business, Roberts was ready to build his empire once the courses were completed.

After buying a service station with a restaurant on Pilley's Island in Newfoundland, Roberts quickly went into acquisition mode adding pharmacies, two pizza franchises, and real estate holdings.

"I designed work systems and started delegating jobs. Along the way I was fortunate to have people working for me who have since become long-term, key people. They are as passionate about my business as I am and run it better than me."

Lesson Two: Assemble your team.

It wasn't all smooth sailing for the young entrepreneur. In 2002, the pharmacy division began faltering when several physicians moved out of the area.

"It forced me to diversify and, due to the problems, we became larger than we ever expected. Sometimes your biggest challenges in business lead to the greatest opportunities. I thought it was a cliché, but now I believe in it wholeheartedly.

"In 2003, I became interested in the Mary Brown's Famous Chicken and Taters franchise. The product was so superior because they used fresh chicken while everyone else's product was mainly frozen. However, I realized they didn't have the resources or infrastructure around it. There was no strategic plan and their marketing was out of date. They didn't even have a website. The brand was on pause and it was amazing it stayed in business as long as it did."

Roberts sensed there was a big opportunity to turn the company around. He met with the owners and noticed they were getting on in years. Greg asked them if they were ready to let go of it and they turned him down flat.

"I traveled to their office every chance I got and kept after them to sell," Roberts recalls, "but they weren't even interested in discussing my offer."

Lesson Three: Be persistent.

By 2006, there were a lot of companies coming forward, interested in buying Mary Brown's, and it looked as if the price of the company was going to be beyond Roberts' reach.

"I had to mortgage everything personally and business-wise and take a huge gamble. I leveraged it all and took out second mortgages. You name it, I did it. It was millions and millions of dollars and I knew if I made a mistake I was going to lose it all."

Was he nervous?

"Nope, I had a plan and I believed in it. I knew the business well and I saw it had a lot of potential. It was like a poker game and I went all in."

Lesson Four: Don't be afraid to take risks.

On February 1, 2007, Roberts flew to Toronto to finalize the deal. Still uncertain how the transaction was going to go, he was on edge when he walked into the first financial institution to get his money.

"I'm used to small town banks," Roberts says honestly. "I was dressed casually, and I assumed if the money was in the account then asking for my multi-million dollar draft wasn't going to be a problem. I didn't realize if bankers in larger centres don't know you, they want to review your account and make sure the previous day's deposits have cleared. They decided to do more due diligence and it took me the entire day to get one bank draft."

With the Mary Brown's ownership group waiting, Roberts knew he had one more bank to deal with before he was able to walk in, lay the money down, and do the deal. He didn't have hours to waste sitting in a bank while they reviewed the accounts, so Roberts decided to turn the tables on the big city bankers.

"I went to one of the most expensive men's clothing shops in downtown Toronto. I spent two thousand dollars on a fancy suit, and told the salesperson the only way I was buying it was if they could tailor it for me right away and deliver it to my hotel room the next morning. They decided to make it happen, so I went and bought shoes, the whole bit. It was the most expensive suit I had ever owned in my life."

The next morning, looking like a million bucks, Roberts walked into the second bank. He only had three hours before the big meeting was to take place at Mary Brown's.

"As I went into bank number two, I walked in as if I owned the place," Roberts says with a smile. "Within ten minutes I had the draft. It was then I realized appearances mean a lot in larger cities."

The meetings and signing the paperwork with the lawyers went on until late in the evening.

"I don't believe a deal is completed until the signatures are done," Roberts says. "I went back to my hotel room and ordered room service. It was around nine at night and as I ate my dinner I finally realized I owned the company."

Greg was thirty-four years old.

"I called my wife and brother to tell them the news. They were all excited for me and then I called my mom. When I told her what I had done she said, 'Now why would you want that?'" Roberts chuckles as he recalls her reaction to the multi-million dollar deal, and then says, "All she wanted to know was if I was okay and if I had eaten dinner."

Mom was looking after her boy. I ask him if he ordered chicken to celebrate closing the deal on Mary Brown's. Roberts pauses for a moment and then says with a huge, roaring laugh, "Nah, I had a big t-bone steak!"

With the ink barely dry on the deal, Roberts began reorganizing and put together a strong executive team.

"Now I had to figure out what to do with it," Greg continues. "We opened new stores and increased the overall business. Growth is currently our biggest challenge, and we've done a lot of new hires in the last year. In many regions, one multinational company is closing stores, so we're moving in and expanding.

We're winning in Canada and while we're still into other industries, going forward our focus will be Mary Brown's.

"We're in the process of developing a new flagship store in South America. We have deals signed in Turkey with a corporate office in Istanbul. Numerous deals in eastern Europe, the Caribbean, and the Middle East are pending, and we've had discussions with many Chinese companies for development there. My goal is to be one of the world's leading quick-service chicken companies within the next five years."

With all the success Roberts has enjoyed, he's never strayed far from his Newfoundland roots.

"My priorities changed when I realized my two little girls were not going to be young forever. I've put my business together in fifteen years and I can tell you it feels like forty. I'll admit I'm tired and I tried to slow down. In 2010, I decided not to buy any more new companies and stay focused on the ones I have. I discovered the tactic didn't work for me because if we're not growing, we're dying. So, I went back into growth mode. In retrospect, I enjoy being busy and expanding."

Lesson Five: Find the right balance.

Roberts lives by simple rules and they work for this business tycoon.

"Work hard, drill down to the root of the problem, and do what you can to make changes. Be candid, listen to everyone, and make the right decisions. Before you get to the challenges, prepare for a rainy day. Remember, in retail, cash is king."

For people looking to build an empire, Roberts has one more piece of advice.

"I credit my background, education, and Chartered Accountant training for getting me to where I am today. I wouldn't have been able to build my company if I wasn't a financial person."

Lesson Six: Remain grounded.

"At the end of the day I don't want to be the richest man in the cemetery. I just want to be remembered as a good person and an even better family man."

Roberts' Business Principles

✓ You need a great idea and an even better plan to make it happen.

✓ Surround yourself with people who are as passionate as you and then listen to them.

✓ Never forget where you're from, and never ask a person to do something you wouldn't do yourself.

✓ Get a great education, keep on learning and taking courses.

✓ Never become arrogant and believe you know it all.

Start Somewhere

Rosalind Chan
International Cake Decorating Artist,
Teacher, and Entrepreneur

When you walk into Sugar Tiers, you are immediately transported into a world of colourful, radiant, edible art. Delicate flowers, finely crafted from infused gum paste, and fondants in every shade of the rainbow are displayed on whimsical cakes surrounded by forty-one flavours of scrumptious macaroons. It's a feast for the eyes and palate as you take in the tasty artistry. Look to the back of the shop and you find a high-tech kitchen area devoted to producing the store's delicious treats and teaching the culinary skills needed to make such stunning creations. Sugar Tiers is co-owned by Rosalind Chan, an international superstar in the cake decorating world.

Years after immigrating to Canada from Malaysia, Chan left a lucrative corporate career to go after her passion full time. Giving up her financial stability and launching her own company was a difficult choice to make.

"I'd worked all my life, so to suddenly not have a salary or a job was nerve-wracking for me."

It has been a meteoric rise to the top of the cake world for Rosalind. She learned her craft at a young age when she visited with her mother in the kitchen.

"My Mom was a beauty therapist trained in Paris but her passion was baking. She was always the recipe maker, and she attended classes where she was introduced to the Wilton Method of cake decorating. She turned out such beautiful cakes."

While Rosalind was inspired, she felt her career was going in another direction. Chan moved to England to study business and law.

"I became an assistant at one of the top legal firms in England. My husband and I had to renew our working permits every year and it was a horrible task because we needed referrals and sponsorship letters, so we looked at other countries. We arrived in Canada on January 2, 1991, when I was seven months pregnant with our second child."

Nine days after Rosalind's son was born she began a new job and worked as an executive assistant at several top corporations over the next nine years. While successful and respected within her industry, the art of cake decorating was pulling at her heart so Rosalind began formulating a strategy.

"When I went home to Malaysia I was asked, 'Why don't you try teaching?' A Wilton distribution company set up classes and I began to instruct. The demand grew and soon I was using all my vacation time to teach. I was flying more than my boss was and I was told, 'As long as your work is done, take paid leave.'"

Her situation had reached a turning point. Married with three young children, Chan and her husband were comfortable in their life and making progress. Was she ready to give up her corporate job and strike out on her own?

"Everyday I asked my husband, 'If I do this, can you feed me? Can you support our family on your own? We have three children to look after. Would you be okay with the household finances?'"

Rosalind grows thoughtful remembering the discussions they had about her future. "He said, 'Try it. If this is what you want in life and it is your passion, you need to go for it.' I realized it was now or never and I wasn't getting any younger. I saw the niche and the potential in the Malaysian market so I took the leap and did it."

She went back to the country where she had grown up and opened a small shop. It took a few months to get the fledgling business going but she felt comfortable leaving the day-to-day operations to her sister-in-law when she returned home to Canada. Despite managing the business from 15,000 kilometers away, Rosalind grew more excited every day.

"No one had ever heard of cake decorating in Malaysia," she recalls. "You never saw a retail store. It started booming because people loved it."

Chan opened up a second store within two years and began looking for opportunities in Canada. When one of her students expressed interest in the business, they decided to form a partnership.

"She and I had worked in the corporate world and yet we had this passion for cake decorating. We opened Sugar Tiers and the business took off."

With the Canadian store doing well, Chan returned to Malaysia where the business was also flourishing. In 1997, Rosalind's abilities were recognized and rewarded when she was named "Wilton Instructor of the Year." More honours and accolades followed.

"I'm now in the Wilton Hall of Fame," she says proudly, "and I was recently inducted into the Presidents Club."

Today, Rosalind is teaching the art of cake decorating in Canada, the U.S., Japan, Korea, China, Indonesia, Singapore, and Malaysia while also taking part in local demonstrations and judging.

"My biggest love is teaching rather than selling. Words can't express the feeling you get when students come up and say 'Thank you for showing me.'"

Chan is now living a life filled with purpose and profitability because she had the courage to take the leap from the corporate world into entrepreneurship.

"I want to continue sharing my love, passion, and skills. I will never stop teaching, even if I can't walk anymore. I can even teach from a wheelchair," Rosalind says with conviction, indicating her career will likely continue long after normal retirement age.

Chan has advice for anyone looking to start their own business.

"Chasing your dream is very important so make sure you build on your passions in life. It's not easy finding a job you love. People go to work every day just to make money. It's so gratifying to earn money and love what you do."

Many don't use the word *dreams* when it comes to business. Rosalind doesn't follow that rule, feeling that visions and goals are what define and drive good businesspeople.

"Never give up on your dream," she cautions. "Always work at it. You may not be able to start big but at least start somewhere. Just don't talk about it – do it. Start on a small scale, start in your basement, or start at home. Just make sure your dreams come true." Rosalind grows thoughtful and adds, "You never stop learning in life. Sometimes you learn from your students as well. The worst thing you can say is, 'I know everything.' The world revolves around new technology. You simply can't afford to take a back seat because something new could be developed the next day. If you sit back and think you know it all, you *will* fall behind.

"I want to add more stores in Canada and branch out to more countries. I want to expand to Thailand, Indonesia, and Australia and share my passion there."

Rosalind is also giving back by reaching out to women's shelters and other charities around the world, teaching people the skills they need to make a career out of cake decorating. Two full scholarships a year are also offered to young girls in Malaysia.

"I feel many people think, 'I've done it – I've achieved everything I set out to do.' In my case I still have a long way to go. There is more to learn and achieve."

Chan is the first Canadian to be certified as a Master Sugar Artist by the International Cake Exploration Society in the United States. She is also writing a book.

Busy and satisfied with her life, she has found a rare balance of making a living at what she's passionate about. For Rosalind Chan, that is the icing on the cake.

Rosalind's Tips

✓ Go to well regarded schools and get as many qualifications as you can.

✓ Get an internship and work with the best.

✓ Take additional courses to build up your skill level.

✓ Network and use social media to introduce yourself to the market.

✓ Develop a business plan and make sure you have enough money to see you through the first year of business.

Vision, Plan, and Execution

Sam Bouji
Chairman and CEO
Global Education Marketing Corporation

"Don't let anyone minimize your dream," Sam Bouji tells me from across a gleaming wood boardroom table. Sam is leaning forward and when I look into his eyes, I see fire and conviction deep in the soul of a man who is determined to make his point.

"You must make your dream come to life everyday. Put it in front of you every minute. Have a vision, a plan, and then execute!"

When you talk to Sam Bouji you quickly learn how passionate he is about business and life. He is a self made man; Chairman and CEO of the Global family of companies, managing three billion dollars in assets for a conglomerate which includes an education trust foundation plus investment, capital, and insurance companies.

Born in Egypt in a town south of Cairo, Sam watched and learned from his father who ran a successful trade and agriculture business.

"My dad came from nothing and he built a great wealth. He had a lot of influence on me and I was so inspired by his achievements and how respected he was within the community. I wanted to be like him."

Bouji began his working life in international trade and manufacturing. He married and became a dad to three young daughters.

"I was in Algeria when the civil war started in 1988. I wanted to be in a peaceful country with a population that wasn't in conflict. Canada had a good reputation, and I decided I wanted to be there."

The Bouji family landed in Canada on March 1, 1989, in the middle of winter and rented a small apartment in Toronto. Within a month he found a job selling water filters. Told to attend a two-day seminar, Sam was excited about joining the company, but he failed the exam.

"I told the president, 'Maybe I don't understand the chemicals, but if you don't hire me you will regret it because I am going to be the number one salesman in your company.'"

Sam kept his promise and less than a month later became their leading seller of water filters. He and his wife bought a house and were in the midst of setting up their mortgage when the company went bankrupt.

"I tried looking for jobs. I sold life insurance but I wasn't happy there. I called my friend who was working with a company called Heritage Scholarship. We went out together and started knocking on doors. I left him and went to the building across the street. I told them the magic word, which was 'scholarship' for their children's education. I was able to make fourteen appointments on my first day. My friend said, 'If you made fourteen appointments in two hours then you will be better than me!'"

Bouji was promoted to sales manager after less than two months on the job, and within a year life was really starting to come together for the new Canadian family. Sam had bought a home, his wife and daughters were happy, and his bank account was growing. Then the unthinkable happened.

"Our house had a pool and it hadn't been closed for the winter. I was in the house with one of my salesmen when my second daughter came in and told me that my oldest had jumped into the pool to go for a swim. I ran to the backyard and jumped in to save her. My salesman heard my screams and jumped in the pool. Both of us were drowning and I blacked out. A neighbour heard our screaming, thought we were fighting, and called the police. They pulled us out of the water and rushed us to hospital."

As Sam reflects back on the tragedy, you can see the pain flood through his eyes when he remembers the dark days that followed. He and his wife sat by their daughter's bed, willing her to open her eyes and praying she would come back to them.

"She was unconscious and struggled for two days. They told me she had brain damage so I knew she was gone."

Sam plunged into despair and was unable to go to work for two months. Finally he realized he had to pull himself together for the sake of his young family.

"However much I beat myself up, I knew nothing would ever bring her back," Sam says quietly. "I decided to focus on the two girls that were still living. God chose me. I decided that I would never forget, but I knew I had to move forward."

Sam went back to Heritage Scholarship and started a sub-agency in his home. By 1993 he was running the top franchise in Canada.

"I was the number one agency in my basement with fifty sales people," Sam says with a huge smile. "My neighbours started to complain about the number of cars that were coming for the Monday morning meetings."

In 1994 Sam bought a section of land and built a new office complex for his growing sales force. Two years later he put in an offer to buy Heritage Scholarship.

"We signed a letter of intent but they reneged. In order to offset it, I set up a new office to accommodate the transition. When they reneged, they compromised and gave me a sub-distributorship.

"In 1998 we split with them and I formed the Global Education Marketing Foundation. It became the twenty-first century investment for education. We now have 112,000 children enrolled. The education savings market is very difficult to work in, but I'm a university grad and I want to see other people have an opportunity to get an education like I did."

Over the years Bouji went on to buy seven other companies and today Global affiliates service 250,000 clients. Looking back, he says one of his proudest achievements are the young people who are either going to university and college or have graduated with no debt due to Global programs.

"22,000 of our students have gone to 37 countries around the world to get their education," Sam says proudly. "Our sales people go to their houses and promise the money will be there. I have delivered."

The Global family of companies currently has over one hundred people on their payroll and fifteen hundred independent sales agents. During the recent recession when companies were downsizing and laying people off, Bouji and Global were hiring.

"It took a financial toll on our company but we knew it would pay off. We were able to get some talented people during that time. We gave many people an opportunity that they appreciate for the long term."

Bouji has a valuable message for aspiring entrepreneurs who have a dream of starting their own business.

"The most important thing is the Laser Beam Strategy. Focus on what you want. People who are distracted and go different directions will not hit their targets or goals. 99 percent of entrepreneurs have failed, in my point of view, because they don't focus on achieving their targets and they don't plan or work very hard. They don't have the discipline.

"People who think they can outsmart and outwork others will not make it. You have to work very, very hard and become the main driver pulling all the people and resources behind you. Everyone will be looking at you. Set the bar high because I don't believe you can achieve anything with very little work. There is no other choice.

"I'm still working twelve hours a day. Every morning I wake up at 6 a.m. because I love to come to work. I tell everyone at my company that if you don't love to work, then hand in your resignation."

Sam stops and laughs, but you can tell he's serious about the commitment and hard work it takes to become successful in life.

"I like to see people helping each other and it brings me a lot of joy when I see my employees helping others and making changes in other people's lives."

Bouji admits he is happy right now. His story is a triumph over tragedy and a true testament to the power of the human spirit. Sam has beaten the odds and succeeded despite suffering the catastrophic loss of a child. He has these final words of advice for people trying to cope with tragic loss.

"I believe deeply in God," he tells me thoughtfully. "The loss of my daughter made me stronger and wiser. I realized I could do one of two things; I could sit there and cry or pick myself up and aggressively rebuild my life. When a person is hit by tragedy or a crisis, it's very difficult but normal life has to continue. You have to find the strength inside to accept the tragedy and continue on with your life."

Sam and his wife had two more children after moving to Canada and he's at a point in his life when he could slow down, however, when the word 'retire' is mentioned the fire suddenly shoots back in his eyes. Retirement is not an option in Bouji's world.

"The older I get, the more productive and wiser I become. I'm not retiring until 2053. That's the year I turn one hundred!"

Bouji's Bullet Points of Success

✓ Don't let anyone minimize your dream.

✓ Have a vision of what you want to do.

✓ Come up with a plan, be patient, and always persevere.

✓ Focus on your targets and be disciplined.

✓ Help others achieve their goals.

Create a Great Team

Ken Fisher
Founder and President of Chatters Canada

Grit and determination. You need it in spades when you're working on the family farm in Unity, Saskatchewan, and competing on the rodeo circuit. On the prairies, you had to be as tough as the animals you were trying to tame or ride. Ken Fisher was, and he competed as an outrider on a chuckwagon team for two years in an event they call *The Half Mile of Hell*. In a race that is wildly exciting and dangerous, thousands of pounds of horses and determined riders gallop around the track bound for the finish line. At night, as the cowboys sat around talking about the day's action, Fisher was always asked what he did outside of the rodeo.

"Well, I'm a hairdresser," Ken would tell them proudly. As he recounts the story from his office in Kelowna, B.C., Fisher breaks into a loud, roaring laugh. "My job was always good for a few chuckles from the guys but I didn't care. I loved it."

Fisher was strong, athletic, and courageous. He was also influenced by an innovative father who instilled a good work ethic in his son.

"Dad was an inspirational trigger for me and someone I always confided in. He also had the creative ability to do remarkable things. When I was six years old, he built a truck for me with a three-speed transmission and a ten horsepower engine you started with a pull. He built a ski-doo before they were even invented. My vision and creativity comes from him. Dad was way ahead of his time."

The family work ethic was also instilled in his older sister Marlene, who became a hairdresser. As a teen, Ken would visit the salon and became intrigued with the business.

"At seventeen, I left home and found a job selling beauty supplies to the salons in Saskatchewan. I did it for three years, then became a hairdresser when I was twenty-one years old.

"I made fabulous money, plus I was dealing with women the whole time," Ken says smiling. "The more time I spent in the shop, the more I realized it was a great opportunity. It was a cash business, the beginning of the beauty retail market, and I loved the women, the fashion, and the hair shows."

The Fishers were also listening to their customers. Unhappy with the shampoo and conditioner they were buying in drugstores, clients began asking Marlene if they could buy their professional "trade only" products and brought their empty bottles into the salon to be filled again.

"When Marlene came up with the retail idea, the first one in North America to pioneer the concept, every manufacturer in the U.S. was suing us, but it made us realize how lucrative it could be."

The lawsuits were dropped when the manufacturers realized there was a new and innovative way to sell their product. It wasn't long before all the beauty industry giants developed professional retail lines.

"I opened my first store in Lloydminster, Saskatchewan, then another in North Battleford and called them Kenneth Blair. We did great business but the market wasn't big enough to sustain itself, so we packed it in and headed south."

Now married with two children and one more on the way, Fisher moved to Regina and opened a salon. He installed a retail division at the front of the store selling high-end shampoo, conditioners, and beauty supplies. Ken worked in the salon and his wife Janine did the books at night. He named the new concept Chatters.

"We mortgaged my house and dumped the whole $35,000 into a promotional marketing campaign. I owned every single sign on the back of all the transit buses, and had the Chatters logo on 70% of bus-stop benches. No one knew who I was, so I'd stand on the corner handing out five-dollar-off coupons. It was new, different, and we quickly became quite successful."

It was 1989, and by 1991 Fisher owned three salons with the retail division placed at the front of the stores.

"That's when I realized I was going to need capital. I brought in several partners and began to franchise. We identified Alberta as a good market and opened a store in Red Deer, which did very well. Lethbridge, Grand Prairie, and Fort Saskatchewan followed, along with several stores in British Columbia."

Expansion was happening, yet it came with a cost. Money was tight and the hours were long and grueling.

"We worked twelve to eighteen hour days, and I traveled close to nine thousand kilometres a month visiting stores and stocking shelves at night," Ken recalls. "Dinner was a raw wiener, a bag of chips, and an apple. My hotel room was twenty-five bucks a night. If we had three people opening a store, we all stayed in the same room to save money. We were barely surviving at home, but I turned all the cash back into the company. Thank goodness I had a strong wife that took care of our kids and supported me while I was building the business."

Starting off in smaller cities and towns was Fisher's key to being profitable right from the outset. He also began assembling a capable team to take his vision to the next level.

"The turning point was having fifteen stores open so we could order volume from manufacturers. The second was partnering with Jason Volk. He brought an understanding of the business and the expertise to put the systems into place. We balance off each other well and have a mutual respect. Robb Bloos was also a key guy for us and a real warrior when we were opening so many stores."

For Fisher and his team, expansion into the big cities was next on the agenda.

Cash flow was critical as Ken knew he'd be paying larger rents. He also had to persuade mall owners to give him a prime retail location.

"They wanted us down the service hallways and it took a long time to convince them we were a retail service. As we began to show the numbers and volume, we captured the attention and respect of the landlords."

It didn't take long for Chatters stores to spring up in Calgary, Edmonton, Winnipeg, Vancouver, and Ottawa. Six stores were opened in Newfoundland and Nova Scotia.

"We've been very fortunate, never had a downside or a year when we didn't experience growth. Our industry is one customers never give up, even in tough times. Secondly, the business has to grow and adapt to the economy. We're in the fashion industry and we have to stay on top as it continues to evolve and change."

Today, there are 115 Chatters stores across Canada, and they recently expanded into Australia. "We found a company that was similar to ours and bought half. It's called Price Attack, and we have 125 stores and a distribution centre."

Fisher has also gone into the men's grooming market by creating Tommy Guns, combining hot shaves and hand detailing with new-school technology. The stores have been an instant hit, featuring in-mirror televisions, iPads for surfing the internet, and arcade games to play while you wait.

"We now have thirteen stores and are adding another ten in the next year. We're looking at expanding into the U.S. and Asia so it will be an international company. There's a lot of room for growth in the men's category. Tommy Guns has tremendous potential."

Fisher is a true entrepreneur having a vision and a concept, then applying the skills and diligent hard work to make success happen. He's also accomplished it all while dealing with Attention Deficit Disorder, a chronic condition that was diagnosed late in his life.

"I was an athlete in school and very competitive," he explains. "I excelled in sports but not on the academic side because I was easily distracted. That's the thing about ADD, I'm always going in so many directions, but my team keeps me focused."

After conducting numerous talks with Fisher, it becomes clear he is a man without ego and takes every opportunity to talk about the accomplishments of the group he has assembled.

"When you have a great idea for a company, make sure you surround yourself with the right people. There isn't anyone who can build and take a company over the top by themselves," he says forcefully. "You have to come to terms with your strengths and weaknesses. Right now we have a young, motivated, aggressive, and accomplished group. I'm also blessed to have a great wife and family. All our kids went into the industry. Two daughters are hairdressers and my son Keenan is heading up Tommy Guns."

With his companies continuing to grow, expand, and franchise, Fisher is also inspiring a new generation of entrepreneurs within his company.

"Several people who started with us now have multiple stores, so at the board level we know we have a big responsibility for people's lives. We have to make sure all aspects of business are looked after for everybody."

Fisher has a message for anyone with thoughts about starting their own company. "You must have passion for your concept or idea, the vision to carry it forward and, most importantly, you must have the strength to get through the bad times.

"There are a million times on the journey you'll want to throw in the towel, saying, 'I don't need this, it's too stressful.' I say, 'Persevere, work hard, and follow your dream.' You also have to believe in yourself. Did I ever believe I'd have over two hundred stores? Absolutely. If I didn't, then we wouldn't be where we are today."

I ask Ken for his final thoughts on where he's been and what the future holds. Fisher pauses for a moment, and then says, "It's funny. In the beginning I thought money is what you measure your success by. Growing older and getting more into the business, you realize money isn't as important. I've realized it's the people, and the new business owners we're creating through our company that brings me the most satisfaction."

"So, if you ask me what color the sky is, I have to tell you, in my world there are no clouds in sight, it's all blue.'"

Fisher's Fortune Five

✓ Have a strong work ethic and passion.

✓ Identify your strengths and weaknesses.

✓ Surround yourself with the right people.

✓ Everything grows and changes. If you sit still you'll get rolled over.

✓ Anticipate what is coming around the corner then figure out what to do next.

Are You a Leader or a Follower?

Ajay Virmani
President and CEO of Cargojet

Ajay Virmani clung to his safety harness as he swung precariously from the fifty-third floor of the Toronto Dominion Tower. It was his first day on the job, and the bucket and window washing equipment they had given him clattered in the heartless winter wind. Glacial ice and water seeped through his jacket, and the dampness from nearby Lake Ontario made him feel miserable and cold. As the buildings in Toronto's financial district swirled around him in a dizzying array of color and lights, Ajay realized his window washing days were over.

The year was 1975, and Virmani had been in Canada only three days. In India he had a Bachelor of Arts with a major in Economics, however, the degree meant nothing in his newly adopted country. "They started me at the top of the building and I had never seen anything that tall in my life," he recalls with a chuckle. "I was so dizzy."

"I got another job fixing speakers and amps at a company in Scarborough for a while," he says quietly. "After that, I found more money working at Midas Mufflers. It was a lot of shift work and welding. My biggest dream was to survive for twelve weeks, then I would pass probation and have a permanent union position. They sat me down after eleven weeks and said,

'We've evaluated your work and have decided this company is not for you.' My dream," he says with a sigh, "was shattered."

Virmani sold vacuum cleaners, freezers, groceries, and life insurance trying to make enough money to live and stay in Canada.

"I sold for Prudential Insurance for about a year and was quite successful, but when I had no more friends left to sell to, I ended up as a customer service agent at a transportation company."

The sales position seemed to be a good fit for Virmani. After working three months in credit and collections, they made him a supervisor, then a customer service manager.

"I progressed well at Cottrell. In those days, there were no computers to handle hundreds of bills of lading, plus the phone calls and telexing. It was quite a cumbersome job."

As Ajay waded through the stacks of paperwork, his hard work was being noticed. By 1982, he was promoted to Assistant Controller and Treasurer. While most people would have been satisfied with their career, Virmani was formulating a plan. On weekends, when others were resting and enjoying themselves, Ajay traveled to New York to get his MBA. Though his intentions were good, it took a financial toll on his family. With two mortgages on his home and using one credit card to pay another, Virmani was in serious debt. As soon as he graduated in 1985, he accepted a job as an Assistant VP at the Bank of Montreal but only lasted one day.

"I realized there was nothing for me in the organization," he says honestly, "so I quit."

Still in touch with Cottrell, they offered him a position as general manager to run their air cargo and shipping business. It was bleeding money, losing one to two million dollars a year, but within twelve months, Virmani had the division breaking even.

Cottrell offered Virmani a partnership then, in 1990, the owner decided to sell the business. The managers had a meeting and agreed to pool their money to buy the company, however, the deal didn't make sense to Virmani.

"I couldn't see paying thirty million for an operation only making five to six million a year. Knowing I had a lot of contacts in the business, I left and started my own international shipping company, figuring if I made $150,000 a year I'd be happy. I knew I didn't want to be part of a leveraged buyout and have bankers running the business."

Within two years, Virmani had exceeded his initial goal and had a five million dollar venture making a half million profit. Going into acquisition mode, Ajay learned First Air Cargo, a competitor, wasn't making any money, and the owner was planning on retiring. He bought it, and within three years was running a ten million dollar operation that was about to get a lot bigger.

"I was on a plane to Calgary," Virmani recalls, "sitting with the CFO of Cottrell going to a golf tournament. I had started my transportation career with them, and the CFO told me it was on the verge of bankruptcy. 'Make the bank an offer,' he said, 'they'll take anything.' I went back to Toronto and, following a few meetings, offered 1.8 million for a company losing millions of dollars. They took it and I have to admit, I was shocked."

Virmani now faced the challenge of financing 1.8 million dollars. So, he sold off the trucking and rail business the day he acquired it, and focused on the air cargo division.

"I got back what I had built," Virmani says proudly.

In 1996, Ajay bought another cargo competitor, TNT, from Australia. The acquisition boosted revenues to fifty million. "By 1999, I had re-named it Fast Air Cargo and CTI. Our group of companies was doing one hundred million in sales and made a profit of ten million a year."

His success hadn't gone unnoticed.

"The president of an American public company called Eagle Global Logistics wanted to buy my company. I told him, 'I don't want to sell my baby.' He was blunt with me and said, 'Your business is not your baby. There is a time to sell and a time to keep it.' He invited me to Houston and put an agreement in front of me. I was told to fill in a price. I had an advisor with me and we put in a silly amount of fifty million. The American changed it to sixty million if I agreed to sell it the same day. I looked at it, made a few phone calls, and then signed it away."

Virmani ran the company for a year while looking for other opportunities, and eventually invested ten million dollars in charter airline, Canada 3000, in July of 2001. Two months later, the World Trade Centre in New York was attacked along with the Pentagon in Washington. The fallout from 9/11 in the airline industry was swift and Canada 3000 went bankrupt.

"With ten million gone, I thought, 'Should I take a tax write-off or should I go after something?' I don't like to lose, so I bought Canada 3000's cargo division out of bankruptcy."

Virmani knew that if a good cargo airline came onto the scene there would be plenty of business.

"Eight air cargo companies had gone bankrupt in the last decade. All the odds were against us but I had a sense of what the market was looking for. They wanted a well financed, stable airline that would provide ninety-nine percent on-time performance. The book value on the planes was ten million each but there were no buyers. So, I bought four planes at $800,000 dollars apiece and renamed the company Cargojet."

"The key was customer service. Previous companies rarely operated on time, so we stressed a sense of urgency. By 2005, we had gone from forty million in sales with a loss of four million, to one hundred million in sales and a ten million dollar a year profit."

The Virmani magic had struck again.

Today, Cargojet has grown to over two hundred million in sales, with close to twenty million dollars in annual positive cash flow and has been named the country's top cargo airline for over ten years. In 2004, Virmani was awarded the prestigious Ernst and Young Entrepreneur of the Year Award, the same year that Cargojet was honoured by Deloitte and Touche as one of Canada's 50 Best Managed Companies.

As he looks back on his rapid rise, Ajay is candid. "Was it luck or hard work? I don't know what the answer is, but I've discovered the harder I worked, the luckier I got." Virmani sits back and laughs, then quickly grows serious again.

"When you're starting out in business, you have to ask yourself three questions. 'Am I the first one offering this product or service? Am I the best one?' If you're not the first, or the best, then you have to ask yourself, 'How can I be different?'

If you don't meet the criteria," he cautions, "then don't get into the business.

"Develop your idea, write it on a piece of paper, talk to people, then fine tune it. Once you identify your goals and objectives in life, I believe you have to become stubborn. If you don't, then you're not going to succeed. You have to believe in yourself, be stubborn and say, 'I'm going to make this happen one way or another.' You have to learn how to take tremendous risks while building a good team around you. If you're a one man band nothing is going to happen by the end of the day because the true success of an entrepreneur is the team of individuals he surrounds himself with."

How you choose your business or product is important too.

"When you get up in the morning you have to love what you're doing. If you hate it, you'll never be successful," Virmani says with considerable conviction.

Other than cargo, Ajay has found one other business he loves: making movies. So far, he has produced *Breakaway*, featuring his son Vinay Virmani and superstar comedian Russell Peters, the upcoming film *Dr. Cabbie*, several Bollywood movies, and the Academy Award nominated *Water*.

"I learned a lot at my MBA school," Ajay says. "The first day they told us about Joseph Kennedy, who survived the stock market crash of 1929 because he went to get his shoes shined. Kennedy apparently said, 'When the shoe shine boys start talking about what stocks to buy then it's time to get out.' Two weeks later the whole market crashed. Don't follow the crowd," Virmani says. "It really registered with me."

The final thought from the award winning entrepreneur?

"Ask yourself, 'Are you going to be a leader or a follower?'"

Ajay Virmani's Secret to Success

S - Sense of purpose.

E - Educate yourself.

C - Creative Ability with your ideas.

R - Responsible. Be accountable.

E - Excellence. Anything you do, make sure you do it well.

T - Time management and Teamwork.

Know Your Worth _____

Trey Anthony
Actress, Playwright,
Producer, and Entrepreneur

Trey Anthony is a force of nature. She is five feet one inch of energy, innovation, creativity, confidence, and greatness. The award winning playwright is best known for her critically acclaimed theatrical play and television show, *da Kink in My Hair*. She is also an actress, comedienne, producer, entrepreneur, speaker, coach, teacher, and author of *The Artist Millionaire*. Trey knows how to make life happen.

"I am very grateful and blessed," Anthony tells me from her production office in Atlanta, Georgia, "but I have big plans for the future."

Before we jump ahead, let's look back on her journey. Born in England, Trey moved to Canada with her mother and brother when she was twelve. The transition into a new life and culture proved to be a turning point for Anthony.

"It was difficult moving from one country to another," Trey admits, "and I was teased quite a bit because I had an English accent. As a teenager, it was difficult to fit in."

Anthony stood in front of the mirror for months practicing how to speak "Canadian." Soon she was adding more accents to her repertoire: Jamaican, Guyanese, and a Scottish brogue. Trey seemed to have a natural talent for mimicking people and the skills the young twelve-year-old learned while trying to fit in to a new country were about to set the stage for her life ahead.

"My family was a big supporter of the arts and my grandparents loved comedy. When we'd all get together, I'd imitate Aunty Zena or my grandmother and I'd make people laugh. I discovered I had good comedic timing."

After taking some classes at the infamous Second City comedy club and school, Trey formed Plaitform Entertainment, a sketch comedy group dealing with issues in the West Indian Community.

"I looked at the entertainment void and realized something was missing for my culture and generation, especially people who had Caribbean parents."

It was the early nineties and Trey and her group started doing shows at a local library. Sold out performances at the Tim Sims Playhouse at Second City caught the attention of the program director at Toronto's Harbourfront Centre.

"It all started happening for us when we performed at the Kumba Black History Festival," Trey recalls. "We had the Harbourfront machine behind us and the venue sat three hundred and fifty people. They put us in their program and we started to do bigger shows every three months."

Trey Anthony had found success on the stage but it didn't always put bread on the table. Following in the footsteps of other struggling artists, she worked at another job doing social work.

"I was a counselor at a shelter helping homeless women and worked with special needs adults on the weekends. I also auditioned for a lot of film and TV roles, getting the stereotypical parts: baby mom, crack-head girl, black-girl-with-attitude. They had seen me as a funny and sassy girl but I needed to be a different black woman on stage. I wanted to do something different, but but no one else could see the vision.

"I brought the idea to my business partners at Plaitform and suggested we do a dramatic play. They said, 'If it ain't broke, don't fix it. Black people don't want to see drama, they want comedy.'"

Shut down by the company she had founded, Trey was frustrated yet determined. At the homeless shelter working the overnight shift, Trey began to write while everyone was sleeping. She wrote for hours and soon the pages of the yellow pad of paper were filled with scripts and ideas. It was starting to take shape and Anthony decided her new play was going to be a series of monologues set in a West Indian hair salon.

"My aunt was a hairdresser. I spent a lot of time there as a child and I knew the business. At the salon, a wide range of women gathered to tell their stories."

The curtain went up on *da Kink in My Hair* in February 2001, at a small venue in Toronto. When they sold out the first night and added another show, Trey knew she had a hit on her hands.

"I saw people's response to the work and the shock around it so I wanted to enter the Toronto Fringe Festival. It cost five hundred dollars and I was so broke I didn't know what to do. My partner gathered all her savings and gave me the money. It was a risk but we knew I was on to something."

da Kink sold out every single night and became the highest grossing play in Toronto Fringe Festival history. They traveled to the U.S. and did the New York Fringe Festival, catching the attention of NBC talent scouts. Anthony says nothing happened from their visit, but she already had a plan in place back in Canada. Trey knew a producer from Mirvish Productions had come to see *da Kink* in Toronto, and she decided to go after the theatrical powerhouse.

"I called Kelly Robinson, the Director of Development, and he told me, 'It was a very handsome production. My girlfriend loved it and was crying, but I just don't get it.' I'm thinking, 'What does handsome mean? My play is handsome?' Trey stops and chuckles at the memory. "I wouldn't let it go and asked for a meeting with Mr. Mirvish. Kelly shut me down again. 'It's not what we're looking for. The play is not palatable for our audience.' He was dismissive but I was relentless and, after several phone calls, he finally gave in, allowing me fifteen minutes with David Mirvish. He obviously was tired of me calling," Trey says, laughing again.

"I assembled box office sales reports, statistics on how many people were buying tickets, the demographics and audience. I even studied Mirvish Production's subscription base and found they were skewing to an older, white demographic. *da Kink* was for a young, diverse, black audience of women twenty to thirty-five. I knew on paper it didn't make sense but I went to the meeting anyway. I gave them all the facts and then said, 'I understand this isn't your usual type of play but your subscription base is going to be dead in twenty years! Don't you want to attract a young and vibrant audience?'

"I stopped and looked over at David Mirvish. He was so shocked his mouth was hanging open. He collected himself and said, 'That's a very valid point young lady.'"

Anthony began her verbal barrage again. "'Everywhere we go, our play sells out. It's young, diverse, and it's going to be your play.' Kelly kept saying, 'I don't get it, I don't get it.' Finally I told him, 'It's not for *you* to get! Your girlfriend was crying and loved the play. Women are buying tickets, and they also buy for their friends and family. It has a repeat audience; people are coming one, two, three times to see it. It makes sense on a business level and it doesn't have to make sense logically. You'll probably never get it!'"

She walked out of the meeting without a commitment, however, fate was about to make a cameo appearance in Trey's life. Mirvish Productions set their schedule for the upcoming year and in the eleventh hour, negotiations for a play they wanted to stage fell apart. Trey received a phone call telling her she had a deal. *da Kink in My Hair* would run for three weeks at one of Toronto's most prestigious theatres.

"I was calm on the phone," Trey admits, "but when I hung up I was jumping all over the place, screaming. My little play was going to be in the Princess of Wales Theatre! I knew in my heart it was going to do well. I said it was touched by the hand of God and I had confidence in its success."

After four weeks of rehearsals, *da Kink in My Hair* opened to a packed house. It was a red carpet event with media and TV cameras. Trey's dad flew in from England and her entire family gathered to support her. Trey's "little play" was a raging success and Mirvish Productions extended its run from three weeks to six months.

"I was on top of the world," Trey recalls. "David Mirvish did an interview saying, 'Audiences are kings and they love *da Kink*. Whether they liked the play or not, money speaks.'"

The play generated so much buzz in Toronto, it was turned into a series running for two years on Global Television.

"I was one of the first African-Canadian women to produce a show on a prime time network. I put black women into a forum never seen before. We were telling stories that had not been seen outside our community. It transformed my life."

Anthony took *da Kink* to San Diego where it was a hit and won four NAACP awards.

"People kept saying, 'You've made it.' I kept thinking, 'I'm still young. I'm thirty-eight years old and this is it?' I told people to quit talking about me in the past tense!"

Anthony kept forging ahead, sponsoring herself to go to the United States and eventually obtaining her green card. Currently, she is in the midst of a U.S. fourteen city tour for *da Kink in My Hair*, doing speaking engagements, school tours, coaching, and writing a self-help book called *The Artist Millionaire.*

"So many people stop me on the street and send emails asking for help. I tell them that no matter what you do, you have to place value on your talent and time. Artists suffer from the 'someone is giving me a chance' syndrome. If a club promoter is still booking you for free after two years, go to him and say, 'Listen. I need to get paid for this.' If not, then you need to walk away. Artists don't know how to negotiate and make money for themselves. They also don't want to hustle. You have to do marketing and put yourself out there. I tell performers to look at who is going to be at the event or gig, and figure out how to promote themselves. It's simple. Use a business card, have a website, create a Facebook page. You can't walk around thinking you're going to make money in your business if you don't have those things.

"When I coach an artist, I tell them to get out of bed every day and say, 'I'm the greatest at what I do.' In Canada, we're bred to be humble about our work. I disagree. I don't want be good, I want to be great and I don't think there's any problem saying it out loud.

"I'm hoping my tour will lead my play to Broadway. I've been in touch with Hollywood producers and I'd love to do a film. I just want to continue to do work I am proud of.

"I am forever blessed."

Trey's Top Tips

✓ Write your goals down.

✓ Work on your goals every day.

✓ Get a mentor.

✓ There is no such thing as failure. They are learning lessons.

✓ Know your worth.

Measure Everything

Robert Meggy
President and CEO
Great Little Box Company

Robert Meggy knows numbers. An accountant and controller by trade, he grew tired of minding the store for other companies and decided to strike out on his own. Putting all the business practices and theories he had learned to work, Meggy took a fledgling company in financial trouble and turned it into a multi-million dollar success story.

In the early eighties, the corrugated packaging industry was controlled by several multinational companies. Robert thought there was room for a regional business to provide faster, more personalized service, so in 1982 Meggy bought the Great Little Box Company out of receivership. At the time, it had three corrugated-packaging presses, two machine operators, and a sales rep.

"I wanted the name so I paid off the debt and I thought we'd do okay," Bob says, as he remembers back to the early days. Then the recession took the knees out of the economy and he watched the sales numbers plummet overnight.

"It was like someone had turned off the tap. During the day I'd be operating the machines, answering the phone, and at night I'd write up orders when we had them. It was a bad time and I lost fifteen pounds."

To make matters worse, Meggy had invested in several rental properties, and as the recession sunk its teeth into the economy, he watched his real estate portfolio spiral down. It wasn't the start in business Bob had imagined.

"It was the wildest swing. My real estate holdings dropped by half. It was hard to get renters and everything was going sideways. It was an ugly, ugly time."

The Great Little Box Company was on life-support and Robert says for several months it didn't look like it was going to survive.

"I decided to sell part of the company to a person who would look after sales. That left me to tend to administration. As an accountant, I'm good at many things but not sales," he says honestly. "I just don't have the personality for it."

It proved to be the right decision. Within a month, business was up eighty percent and GLBC made money for the first time since Meggy took over. By the end of 1982, the company was showing signs of life and he eventually bought out the salesman to obtain sole ownership.

In the following years, Bob gently nursed the company along, and was rewarded with steady growth and profits. By 1995, he was rapidly running out of space for his expanding business.

"We were renting space in three buildings and forklifts were going up and down the alleys," Meggy recalls. "It was ugly and inefficient. We needed space, and rent was a big factor."

Bob found a building at a good price and went to the bank to get financing. Two days before closing, the financial institution called to say there was a problem.

"Someone decided to put the debt of the building against the operating line. I went over there and was told purchasing the building would be detrimental to my business. I drove to a credit union and within a half an hour had moved all my accounts."

The Great Little Box Company still wasn't out of the woods. The credit union was willing to give him seventy-five percent of the purchase price. Time was running out and Meggy only had a few days to come up with the rest.

"I had to borrow hundreds of thousands of dollars from friends, and friends of friends," Meggy says quietly. "I gave them fifteen percent interest for two years and repaid it as soon as I could. I've never looked back since."

When it came time to expand again, Bob put the building on the market and watched with glee when a bidding war broke out. When the dust settled, the property had sold for over one million more than he was asking. Meggy turned the profit back into the company and bought ten acres of land near the Vancouver Airport, then built a 250,000 square foot facility.

"Cash-wise we're well protected," Bob says. "We have good equity, so as a business owner I don't have to worry. Not having access to cash will take a company down. When running a business it's important to remember cash is king, you must protect it at all times, and have a backup."

You should also know when to expand your portfolio. In 2008, Meggy knew a recession was coming. It was long overdue, and with the collapse of the banking sector in the U.S. it was only a matter of time before the effects hit Canada. Robert knew the time was ripe to start expanding the company.

"We looked at all our competitors and ended up buying seven. We acquired shipping supply businesses, label manufacturers, smaller box companies, and our main foam competitor. It worked out great for us."

Meggy says having the right team in place is critical to a company's success.

"People are your number one asset. We conduct seven to eight interviews for each person we hire. We want to find out who the real person is and we want nice people. A moody employee can drag down a whole department. It's important everyone works well together. You'll lose $50,000 to $100,000 if you don't choose the right person."

Bob makes sure every employee hired cares as much about the Great Little Box Company as he does by holding monthly meetings where they review the income statement and balance sheet.

"We run an Open Book Management. Not many companies operate that way. At our monthly meetings, we go through everything and talk about where we are financially. I've seen more companies where people go to work and there's big a sign on the door saying *Receivership*. The employees have been spending money and the owner isn't sleeping at night due to the fact everything is going so badly, yet no one is told anything. Run an open book," he says forcefully, "so people know what's going on."

Meggy's employees are also clear on their yearly goals and expectations. An attainable goal is set, and if it is met the whole company goes on a trip together to Las Vegas or Mexico. Along with Open Book Management, Bob has also set up a program where a percentage of the profits is split equally with everyone in the branch every month.

"I've had employees come into my office and ask if the sales people are working hard enough," Bob says with a laugh. "I know everyone is talking about it on the plant floor because they're getting a cut and are seeing their monthly reward. We're also honest. People say you shouldn't give your employees bad news because they'll quit. I say BS; the staff all need to know what's going on. If they like the company they will try harder and take more interest in their job.

"The number one thing employees want is recognition and appreciation, so we encourage their feedback. When you measure and hire better people it shows you care more."

Today, the Great Little Box Company employs 250 people and is on target to make over forty million dollars in sales. Meggy credits all the company's success to assembling the right team.

"I run it as if everyone is a group of friends. I walk around the plant every week and talk to as many as I can. I visit our branches. You spend most of your waking hours with the people you work with. Enjoy them because it makes a huge difference. When you run an open book you sense a trust in the company and the staff care more. Profit sharing has really made a difference."

The accountant who became an entrepreneur becomes animated when he talks about the most important business practice he's learned over the years. If you want to be successful in business, Meggy says to measure everything.

"Have you ever met a golfer who doesn't keep score? It's no different in a company. Measure the number of cold calls, sales, machines, speeds, and how many pieces per hour. It all comes down to efficiency and success. In the end, you'll care more and take an interest. It makes a huge difference."

From this accountant, that's advice you can take to the bank.

Meggy's Measurements for a Well Run Business

✓ Set yearly goals.

✓ Protect your cash.

✓ Realize people are your number one asset.

✓ Encourage feedback from your employees.

✓ Measure everything.

The Science of Business

Dr. Monique Haakensen, Ph.D., P.Biol.
President and Principal Scientist
Contango Strategies

"I never meant to become an entrepreneur. It was an accident, but I'm glad it worked out," Monique tells me from her laboratory in Saskatoon. She grows silent and then says with a laugh, "I never meant to become a scientist either!"

Haakensen grew up outside of Prince Albert, Saskatchewan, on an acreage where her love for the outdoors was cultivated.

"We didn't have a ton of money," she recalls, "but we went camping, fishing, and I worked in the garden. I was interested in the outdoors and I loved nature."

Monique did well in school and seemed destined to become a doctor. She enrolled in pre-med courses at the University of Saskatchewan but immediately knew it was a mistake.

"For starters, I faint when I see blood," Monique says, and then laughs even harder before she turns serious again.

"As a doctor, you give people a drug when they have a symptom. I wanted to know why I had a desire for a different level of understanding. It was then I realized medicine might not be the right fit for my interests.

"In my second year of university, I took a microbiology class as an elective. At that time, I had no idea what being a scientist was about. I thought they sat in laboratories all day looking into a microscope, but this course opened my eyes to what being a scientist meant. I like working as part of a team and when I discovered science was collaboration and problem solving, I decided to move in that direction."

During her graduate studies, Haakensen also learned how one sector of science is applicable to another.

"In science you would think everyone is aware of the research happening across various fields, but there isn't much communication. For example, there are technologies in health care directly applicable to environmental work, so I started to explore ways to apply those technologies."

That philosophy led her to explore jobs studying microbial impacts on mining byproducts and the environment. It proved to be pivotal for Haakensen.

"I loved being on site at a mine, collecting samples and seeing the application of what I was doing. I was then offered a job as a government scientist where I spent a year bridging different disciplines of science for environmental projects."

However, it didn't take long for Monique to realize the government employee lifestyle wasn't a fit. Feeling disillusioned by her choice to be a scientist, she wasn't sure what to do. Haakensen had several job offers and even entertained the idea of helping out at her husband's financial firm. Then a company pursuing technology she had patented for the biofuel sector contacted her, and suddenly it was decision time.

"Was I going to accept a comfortable job working for someone else or take a huge risk and open a laboratory?" Monique reflects somberly. "It's not only incredibly hard to open a lab but it is also ridiculously expensive. My husband encouraged me to do it and we put up our savings."

With family money on the line she knew there was a lot at stake.

"There is no incentive like having to use your own money to keep you focused on things. It's terrifying. When you talk about being bold, you have to believe in what you're doing, know your markets, and what you're planning to do. There's no point to going into business if you think it will fail. You must be aware of the downside but not dwell on it. Prevent it and focus on the growth."

Monique named her company Contango Strategies and set up a lab in Saskatoon. It is the only company providing cold climate constructed wetland treatment pilot facilities and services in North America.

"If you're going to build a mine," she adds, "You have to prove the water coming off the operation isn't going to hurt the environment. We have the ability to treat water in a natural way. We provide a service that allows our clients to obtain their license to operate, save millions of dollars in operational costs, and help the environment.

"We are also one of the few genome sequencing services of its kind in Canada," Monique tells me proudly. "Over the past year and a half, we have developed technologies that allow us to take samples of dirt or water and identify every microbe. No one else offers that type of service."

Six months after startup, Haakensen was able to put the family investment back in the bank, however, a few months later she needed to dip back into their savings.

"It was cash flow," Monique explains. "I had contracts and money coming in the door but I had to pay the bills in between. Cash is king and you need ready money to keep your business going. Until you have a comfortable cushion you have to be willing to put it in yourself."

Haakensen admits being a businessperson is totally different from being a scientist. "You are responsible for everything including your employees. There are huge challenges and stresses in running your own business, but I love it. If you don't enjoy it then business isn't right for you.

"I talk to a lot of students and I tell them there is no magic recipe for success. You have to know the so-called rules, break half of them, and be aware of everything you do.

"If you're not in it to make money you're not a business, you're a hobby. There are a lot of things that are fun to do where you gain experience, but it's not a business if your main goal isn't to generate a profit."

Haakensen also has an opinion on getting too comfortable once your business is running well.

"Don't be complacent. Things can change, market conditions can change, or a competitor could move in. Always have alternate plans and backups for your backups.

"Business isn't for the faint of heart. I knew it was going to be difficult and in a way it was even scary at times. You have to be ready to handle it all. Last month I worked four hundred hours. I'm not complaining. I actually enjoyed it. How many people can say they spent four hundred hours last month doing something they love and are passionate about? People who aren't entrepreneurs don't usually understand the concept of working that many hours. People say you have to get a life. Well, it is my life and that's what I've chosen. Do what you love and make sure it's the right balance for you."

In less than two years of operation, Contango Strategies has secured numerous large multi-year contracts. They're also getting referrals, repeat clients, and word of their unique and innovative services is spreading quickly within the marketplace.

"We're continuing to evolve and are fortunate our sector is growing. This year we have expanded to the Yukon, Northwest Territories, and Alberta. In addition to our core focus on mining, we are now doing more oil and gas work. As a result, we have doubled our lab space, added 1,800 square feet of greenhouse space, and an outdoor pilot facility."

So far, the success factor is rising for Contango and Haakensen, but she is prepared for any downfalls or speed bumps coming her way.

"One of my favorite quotes is from Thomas Edison who said, 'I have not failed, I just found ten thousand ways that won't work.' In science, you may fail multiple times a day; however, it is those failures that lead you to discover what works. The same goes for business. Realize it's not failure, it's just a stepping stone of the learning process."

The final thought from this business-savvy scientist?

"Learn from everything," Monique says with a smile, "and keep moving!"

Haakensen's Success Formula

✓ Relationships

They are everything in business and that is where all your referrals come from. Your reputation is everything.

✓ Tenacity and Persistence

Learn from everything and keep moving. Be flexible enough to know when you have to change and bold enough to take risks.

✓ Listen...

- to your clients - they will tell you what product or service they need from you;
- to your team - they will let you know where you have to improve and optimize your processes;
- to your family and friends - they are your reality check.

✓ Honesty

Always be honest and ethical with yourself, your team, and clients.

✓ Cash flow

Successful businesses live and breathe with cash flow, not earnings. You always need to pay your employees and bills on time, but don't always assume all your customers will follow suit.

Work Hard and It Will Work Out

Wayne Purboo
Founder, President and CEO
QuickPlay Media Inc.

"It's all or nothing being an entrepreneur. It's a very risky proposition."

Wayne Purboo is a quiet and serious man, however, there is no question the passion for his company runs deep in his veins. Purboo says the secret to success is simple and people have known about it for years.

"My father was a man of few words, but he always told me, 'If you work hard, it will work out.' It was his answer for everything and it became part of the fabric of who I am."

Purboo was born in Jamaica, and moved with his family to Toronto when he was a young child. Wayne was a good student and excelled in sports, telling me he wore a tracksuit to school every day.

"I played a lot of sports and did well in basketball and volleyball. I was named Athlete of the Year, and followed the coach of my Ontario Select team to McMaster University where I studied computer sciences."

Along with sports and attending school, Wayne knew the value of having a good job.

"I did it all, from paper routes to clerking in a bookstore and working in machine shops with my dad. I did all kinds of things and worked throughout university."

With his future ahead of him, the athlete and student had no idea a dump truck was about to change his life forever. Driving to school on a wintry afternoon after visiting his parents, Wayne was involved in a collision. The wreck was so bad they had to use the Jaws of Life to cut him from the car. Wayne awoke in the hospital with a broken hip, and the extent of the damage was so bad it quickly became clear his days as a star athlete were over.

"It's scary when you can't walk and you're used to being so active."

Stoic and resigned to his fate, Wayne went home for a few months to recover. Sitting in front of his computer, he built a software application for a friend in the recruiting business. Once the database was completed, Wayne knew the direction he wanted to pursue.

"Windows was starting to take hold," Purboo explains. "There was a huge vacuum of talent and a need for people to work in the field. I went back to school and earned my computer science degree. In the summer, I found a job-posting for a company opening in Toronto. Their main office was in Silicon Valley and I told them, 'Look, I don't have everything you need but I'm willing to work very hard and throw myself into this.' They had a lot of applicants, however, I was fortunate and they hired me. I was determined to stand out."

The company was called NCD – Network Computing Devices – and Judy Estrin and Bill Carrico were about to take the company public. Estrin, who has made Fortune Magazine's list of fifty most powerful women in business numerous times, was one of Silicon Valley's original entrepreneurs. While getting her Master's degree from Stanford, Judy worked with Vint Cerf, a computer science pioneer often called the "Father of the Internet." Her credentials were impeccable and Wayne was about to learn from the best.

"They liked me a lot and I advanced quickly. I was always making trips back and forth and my responsibilities kept increasing. I learned about IPO's, stock purchase plans, venture capital, and financing companies. We were a small company exposed to a lot of opportunity and it gave me the bug to be an entrepreneur. In Silicon Valley, they believed they could change the world, so when I came back to Toronto I started looking for opportunities."

Purboo teamed with Kevin Kimsa in 1994 at Solect Technology Group. They began building networks for phone companies in the Caribbean, catching the attention of telecommunication giant Sprint. Expanding further, they began reselling their technology to other jurisdictions. For six years the hours were long, but in 2000 their efforts paid off when they sold the company for 1.2 billion dollars.

"We had several big owners, however, we held a minority stake and did quite well. I started to think about what I was going to do next and QuickPlay was born."

Going back to what he had learned with Judy Estrin in Silicon Valley, Purboo began looking at the way premium content was acquired and consumed on the internet. There seemed to be a gap in the infrastructure for large pay TV operators and their capability of delivering to internet-connected devices.

Purboo had stayed at Solect to oversee the transition, but in 2003 he decided it was time to move on. He pitched his idea to Raja Khanna, who owned an online digital company called Snap Media Corp. The entrepreneur bought into the proposal, and then Purboo had to break the news to his wife.

"I told her we were going to take a huge hit financially and my salary was going to be ten percent of what I was currently making. I was honest and said we didn't know how it was going to turn out, but she was supportive and encouraged me to pursue it. We'd been together for a long time and she knew I was going to give it my all."

Purboo moved into the Snap Media offices and hired a team of developers and programmers. Wayne had made several key contacts with pay TV operators while at Solect and began to talk to them about his new technology.

"We launched the first mobile video service in Canada in September 2004, and signed Rogers and Telus to contracts. The first day, people watched one hundred videos and it was incredible."

Today, QuickPlay has seventy million views a month around the world, with people watching everything from full length movies to live TV channels on IP-connected devices. Communication giants Verizon, AT&T, Rogers, and Bloomberg use QuickPlay technology, and in ten years the company's revenues have soared. They are a privately held company, however, Purboo says he has plans to take QuickPlay public.

"Some say we're ready but I want to get to one hundred million in revenue before we IPO. We're on a good trajectory to get there. Last year, we did a buyout of our venture capital partners with Madison Dearborn, a private equity firm out of Chicago. We've re-capitalized the company and are looking forward to continued growth."

It hasn't always been a smooth journey for Purboo and QuickPlay.

"The Global recession in 2008 and 2009 stalled a lot of plans for us and our customers," Wayne admits. "We're a couple years behind where we thought we'd be because growth stopped. They were tough years and we did a round of financing we probably wouldn't have done had the crisis not happened. We've always had a strong view of the future to focus and make investments, so we bought a facility in San Diego to support our aspiration to deliver premium content. It was tough to convince our board to buy it, but now we're reaping the benefits."

Revenue and success are good to have when running a company, but Purboo says he's sacrificed a lot to ensure upwards growth for QuickPlay.

"If it was easy, everyone would be doing it. This is work," Purboo says forcefully. "The biggest mistake entrepreneurs make is not focusing the limited resources they have on the most critical items. I've seen companies concentrate on a website, but if you're not selling from it then it's not critical. I feel the most important factor is to acquire great talent right away. In my industry, you have to find like-minded people to share your passion and work hard in order to make these things happen. As an entrepreneur you have to figure out where you should spend money to grow and succeed. Figure out what you have to do and then get it done.

"As long as you love what you do, you can take the ups and downs. I never know when I wake in the morning if I'm going to have a good day. It's all about managing the highs and lows and staying focused."

Purboo is proud of what he's accomplished so far in life, however, money and success don't mean as much to him as the happiness of his family.

"I'm a dad first to my three boys. I can't play as many sports as I used to, so they fulfill the competitive side of me. I'm a cheerleader and a proud parent in the stands watching them play hockey. There's something to be said about sports; it's a great equalizer. It doesn't matter how much money you have or where you come from, you have to perform.

"My mother and father always told me to work hard. They set an example, so I'm doing it for my boys. I've become conscious of the legacy I'm leaving behind so I am instilling a work ethic in my sons. They don't have to struggle as hard as I did but they still need a little bit of dirt under their fingernails."

As Purboo looks ahead he sees a bright future for himself and QuickPlay.

"I believe I can be more successful than I am now. Part of being an entrepreneur is always thinking you can do better. I'm very critical of myself, however, I believe I can exceed my expectations."

I ask Purboo how he plans on achieving his goals.

"By working hard," he replies simply.

For all of us, that's the bottom line.

Purboo's Pivotal Points for Prosperity

✓ Passion. Be passionate about your endeavour.

✓ Knowledge. Be a thought leader in the market you intend to conquer.

✓ People. Surround yourself with like-minded people who share your passion.

✓ Agility. Be prepared to change plans if your assumptions are incorrect.

✓ Focus. Limited resources must be efficiently consumed to get the most leverage possible.

Never Give Up

Kam Ko
Founder and President
Kobotic Ltd., Inventor and Artist

"If you give up right now, you will give up on everything for the rest of your life." Kam Ko stared into the eyes of the survival camp instructor and realized his life was about to change. The twenty-three year old was taking part in a program called Outward Bound, a wilderness training group originally formed to train soldiers for war.

"We were taken to an isolated island off the coast of Hong Kong in the middle of winter, and given a sweater, swimming trunks, and a poncho. I was allowed one jug of water, a handful of rice, and three matches. I knew people had been injured, become sick, and even died while taking part in the program, but I wanted to complete the course. We simulated being in a shipwreck, even jumping into the freezing cold ocean, and after thirty days of intense training and hardship I knew I was capable of surviving anything."

With a new outlook on life, Ko went back to the power plant in Hong Kong where he worked as a welding technician. Kam had a natural talent for joining metal and had climbed quickly in the company, supervising two hundred welders by the time he was nineteen. Now, four years later, Ko realized it was time to get a university degree. With only two schools in the area, his chances of being accepted were slim so he decided to move to Canada.

Kam arrived in Toronto in 1972, with one suitcase and enough money to last a week. He had a friend who had immigrated before him so at least he knew one person in the big city. Fully qualified as a welder, instructor, and supervisor, Ko applied to a number of companies. His experience meant nothing in Canada and they all refused to hire him.

"They looked down on me due to the fact I didn't have any Canadian experience. I thought to myself, 'I can survive Toronto.' So I went back to school."

Never give up.

Ko found a part-time job at a security company counting deposits at night. Attending school during the day, his rent was high and money was tight.

"I went to Kensington Market and bought a big bag of chicken wings for one dollar. I cooked them all at one time and they became my breakfast, lunch, and dinner for an entire week. Life was hard but I graduated with honours."

Learning his sister was working as a nurse in Montreal, Kam packed up a suitcase and moved east, applying at Dominion Bridge in Lachine, Quebec. Securing an entry-level welding job, he moved up quickly within the company. Within six months he was offered a job in the research department and found his first mentor.

"Mendoza was a big guy," Ko recalls. He was 6'3" and I was only 5'7". I called him Grandpa and he taught me a few tricks. In a lab you can't make any mistakes and my boss was always standing behind me looking over my shoulder, making me nervous. Mendoza looked after me and we became good friends."

Kam learned every job in the lab and became indispensable. It wasn't long before he was promoted to the post of senior technologist along with Mendoza.

Ko also became friendly with a budding young pharmacist. Edna was an energetic and attractive girl who was a friend of his sister. They began dating and stayed together even when she moved with her family to Boston.

"All the money I earned at Dominion Bridge was spent on phone calls and driving to Boston to see Edna," Kam chuckles.

Four years passed before Ko was able to start pursuing the university degree he had come to Canada to obtain. Switching to part-time employment with Dominion, he went into survival mode again. Ko had a goal and was finally rewarded with a mechanical engineering degree.

Life switched from survival to lightning opportunity. Accepting a job at The Welding Institute of Canada, he moved back to Ontario and obtained his Master's degree. Kam also married Edna and they settled in Richmond Hill.

"Bill Davis, the premier of Ontario at the time, had funded six high tech centres to compete with offshore imports. The Ontario Robot Centre approached me and I accepted. They wanted to introduce new technology to industry in the province and make production lines more efficient. Company reps came in to see the robots and talk to us about their projects."

It proved to be a turning point for Kam Ko. He loved the job, and was fascinated with robotics.

"Edna was a pharmacy manager and didn't want to move, so I commuted three hours every day. I never gave it a second thought. The first time I saw the machines I said, 'wow.' I never thought I'd own sixty of them one day."

New opportunities opened for Ko. He taught robotics at a college and accepted jobs at auto-part manufacturing giants Van-Rob Stampings and Magna International. Robotics became a passion and, when applied with his knowledge of welding, Kam Ko became an expert people went to for answers.

"A salesman from a welding supply company came to see me. One of his customers had received one thousand welded auto parts but they rejected three hundred. I met with his customer and offered to do some test welding. When I returned the parts, they gave me a purchase order on the spot. Now I was faced with a new challenge; I had to start my own company."

Ko had mixed emotions about the new opportunity and was plunged into a quandary.

"I had never intended to start a business, only to invent things. I wanted to make them better and more efficient."

Ko worked out the numbers and realized he needed a small shop. Walking into his bank, he applied for funding.

"They told me that I had no experience in business or with money and they refused me. I went to Edna and we decided to find the financing ourselves. I called a former colleague in Boston and bought a used robot. 1993 was an exciting year."

The hard work started. Ko had to produce two thousand car parts a month while keeping his job at Van-Rob Stampings.

"As soon as I finished for the day, I took off my tie and put on my blue lab coat and went to work in my shop around the corner. During the day I was a Chief Engineer but at night I was a labourer, salesman, and janitor."

He also had to become a mechanic.

"There were times when the robot stopped working at 2 a.m. in the morning. With the delivery truck set to pull into the loading dock at 8 a.m., I had to troubleshoot and fix it quickly. I remember pleading with it, 'Please robot, please work!' I never quit and the robot wasn't allowed to either."

Never give up.

Kam named his company Kobotic Ltd., and as production increased so did the purchase orders. Ko was working every day before work, during lunchtime, and in the evening. Even Edna was pressed into service, taking off her white pharmacy jacket at night and putting on a blue one to make car parts.

After a year, Kam was able to quit his job and work full-time at Kobotic. Former employers Van-Rob and Magna became his customers and he added six more robots.

"After my first experience with the bank I didn't want to go back. I put all the profits into building my business. Unfortunately, I acquired several bad customers unable to pay their bills. Due to my inexperience I trusted them and, as a result, learned many tough lessons. Some went bankrupt and others cheated me. I was job hungry and underpaid but I kept going."

Never give up.

By 2007, Kobotic had thirty employees operating as many robots in a twenty-thousand square-foot facility.

"Every time I made money, I bought new robots. I never borrowed from the bank and that's why I was sleeping at night. There was a downturn in 2008, and many of the jobs I was promised never happened. If I had borrowed money from the bank and the machines were not generating money then I would lose sleep. Instead, I owned it all and was only answerable to myself."

With Kobotic rolling along, Ko found the time to focus on his true passion, inventing machines and goods to make life more comfortable and efficient.

"A pharmaceutical friend showed me an I.V. bag with a needle pushed into a bottle of medicine. Nurses were getting carpal tunnel syndrome and they asked me to develop a better way. I invented a Vial Docking Station capable of inserting four bottles of medicine at a time, replacing the work done by human hands. It also uses all sizes of bottles compared to the U.S. machines that can only accommodate two medicines of the exact same size."

Ko got a call from a relative in Australia wondering if his scientific mind might be able to help them.

"My niece is a dentist and was suffering back pain from leaning over her patients, so I developed a front leaning support chair. A friend invited me to take my invention to a tradeshow in Germany and people loved it. They called it revolutionary, and had never thought about sitting in a chair offering support from the front. It gave my business a great boost and today I have chairs all over the U.S., Europe, and Australia. It's also used in a dental training department at a college in Canada."

The Kobo chair and the Vial Docking Station have been patented and Kam is busy working on several new inventions.

"After twenty years in business I wanted to do something different, so I sold Kobotic last year. It was a multi-million dollar deal so I was happy, although I am staying on for two years as the company transitions to the new owners.

"As I look ahead, I want to develop the Kobo chair further. I also enjoy traveling and building new things, painting, and making metal sculptures. I don't see myself ever retiring."

As our time together comes to an end, I ask Kam for his final thoughts on life and business.

"Trust in what you believe in and go for it. Find a good person who can help you because you can never achieve everything yourself. A good leader needs good followers. Find your people and then trust them with all your heart. Never cheat people, and understand there are no shortcuts in life. Finally, I tell people to be persistent and always remember to never give up."

Kam Ko's Conclusions on Business

✓ Have a vision of what you want to do and stick with it.

✓ Give your vision the action it needs to make it happen.

✓ Don't rely on banks if you don't have to. You have your family and friends to turn to.

✓ Take small steps in business because they add up.

✓ Never give up.

Believe

Jennifer Carlson
Founder and President of Baby Gourmet

On the inside of Jennifer Carlson's right wrist is a small tattoo. It says *Believe*, and it serves as a daily reminder for the Calgary businesswoman to remain focused and to never lose faith in her vision and goals.

"I was in my car a lot in the early days," Jennifer says, "so it was a constant reminder to keep moving forward. You need to believe in what you're doing and know you can overcome anything."

Jennifer launched Baby Gourmet out of her kitchen in Calgary and, in a few short years, has taken the company across Canada and into the U.S. with sales of over seven million dollars a year.

"We're feeding kids delicious foods they love to eat so moms can feel good. I always trust my intuition and it is what's taken me forward."

Being an entrepreneur was always in Jennifer's blood. Carlson started a dog walking business when she was nine, sold homemade baking to campers in the nearby Rocky Mountains at the age of twelve, and put together a plan for a new restaurant when she turned thirteen. "I loved business. It's what drove me. I went to school and received a diploma in marketing; however, I never finished my degree. I found I worked better as a hands-on person rather than sitting in a classroom listening to lectures."

The birth of a daughter proved to be a turning point for Jennifer and put her on the path to creating Baby Gourmet. Not happy with the quality of products found in supermarkets, she began to make baby food from scratch. Within two weeks, all the moms in her baby support group were paying Carlson to prepare food for their children too.

"I thought the best place to start my new venture was at a high-end farmers market. I started selling my food and doing market research. I needed to know what moms were looking for and how much they were willing to spend. I did it for two years, developed great knowledge about feeding babies, and built a very successful local brand."

Carlson shocked everyone when she shut down the new company. It wasn't for lack of success; she knew it was time to go bigger.

"I knew I was working *in* the business, not working *on* it. So, I stopped selling and began looking at the big picture. I believed every mom and baby deserved good food but I needed to reach them on a mass level."

That's when the hard work began.

"Everyone loved the idea and product, however, they knew I was lacking in execution and capital. I went down every avenue and put the word out on the street that I was looking to bring in management. With my newborn strapped to my body in a baby carrier, I was exhausted and thought, 'I can't do it anymore,' but I had to keep going."

Carlson began networking and investigated financial resources available in Alberta. She developed a solid business plan with promising numbers and future innovation. The new company looked great, yet people wanted to hold her back.

"A lot of people in the industry said to start small and grow organically. I thought about it and realized I'd never reach the number of moms and babies I wanted to. It was my goal to start at the top, so my first presentation was to Walmart."

Carlson had the product, the packaging, and a manufacturer in place, then went out and nailed the pitch in front of the Walmart executives. Climbing into the car after the meeting, her cell phone buzzed with a new message. The Walmart buyer was emailing a contract.

"I was still in the parking lot," Jennifer recalls. "I looked at my sales guy and said, 'Did that just happen?'"

Baby Gourmet was born and went into a rapid growth phase. What started out as a trial with Walmart, turned into nationwide distribution, expansion in the U.S., and annualized revenue of six million dollars.

"My children helped me develop recipes and my son's picture went on the packaging. I was on the road a lot and it was difficult, but I made sure to spend a lot of quality time with them."

In 2011, Carlson was awarded one of the top honours in business when she captured the Ernst and Young Emerging Entrepreneur of the Year award.

"When I heard my name being called, I had an overwhelming sense of emotion. Walking to the stage, I thought back to buying my first jar of baby food and thinking, 'One day, I need to have *my* food in this store.' To go from stirring pots, being the mom of a newborn and toddler, to winning an award was surreal."

Carlson was on top of the world and had it all, but had no idea what she had carefully built was about to slowly crumble.

"I hired an executive team to run the organization, then I found out there were people with ulterior agendas. Our CEO wasn't looking after the company and had structured Baby Gourmet around himself. He was used to running a company with deep pockets, so he over-extended us and was pursuing expansion into other countries before we had solidified our plans in North America. We lost a lot of money in 2012.

"I tried to question him and the board. No one was doing anything about it. I knew we were heading for a cliff and felt as if I was living in a John Grisham movie. The board was split and our CEO had veto power." Jennifer pauses for a moment and collects herself before continuing the story.

"They criticized me for being too emotional. I was angry, and reminded everyone our brand was built on emotion and love. I felt like a mother bear protecting her young. Nothing I said made any difference. They all thought I should be removed. I was almost pushed out, and the company was on the verge of going under."

Jennifer looked down at the inside of her wrist and stared at the small tattoo.

Believe.

It was time to save the company.

"I brought in one of my key investors and we pulled together a concept the board couldn't deny nor turn down. I informed them it was their fiduciary duty to state the CEO and executive chairman were wrong. They agreed. Within twenty-four hours we managed to hire a new CEO, put in a new executive chair, restructure the board, and raise three million dollars."

Company saved. Believe it.

"Our sales are great and we're capturing more market share," Jennifer tells me. There is an immediate change in Carlson as she becomes happier; however, a steel-coated confidence emerges in her voice as she continues. "We're in all major retailers in Canada and we're still in the U.S. The challenging part right now is managing the growth. We're raising capital, obtaining resources, and looking at hiring more people.

"We've launched Kids Gourmet, and I've turned my innovation and focus to product development. From babies to toddlers to kids, it's very exciting and I see a big opportunity there. Parents are looking for healthy snacks for their kids so we recently launched *Squoosh*, our new brand which features a full serving of fruits and vegetables in four flavours."

Carlson's candor about Baby Gourmet's recent struggles is refreshing. She says it's important for new business owners to learn from the trials of others.

"I'm real and honest. I want people to know what is expected and what can happen. It's challenging being an entrepreneur. You're told to hire people to fill the gaps and lead the operational end of a multi-million dollar company. You carefully bring people in and trust them, but things can still go wrong. It's part of the journey of being an entrepreneur. You are always learning."

Carlson also has a message for women in business. Despite the strides made by females in the last three decades, she warns there is still a double standard in the corporate world.

"Men are positioned to be seen as strong and confident. Yet a woman who is passionate and dynamic is seen as threatening, selfish, and angry.

"It made me furious to be called emotional. I don't cry. In fact, I've been to therapy to learn how to cry. I was on the verge of tears in the board room defending myself.

"It's a double standard and I will not change the way I am. I'm strong and confident. There will always be criticism, but I choose not to listen to it. The odd time it breaks me down but for the most part, I tune it out."

Jennifer pauses, then grows thoughtful about what she wants to share with future entrepreneurs.

"Running your own business takes confidence and risk, but have persistence. You may hit a wall, but you have to push through because nothing in life worth having is easy to obtain."

Carrying her business battle scars proudly, the tattoo on Carlson's right wrist has taken on a greater meaning.

"Even when I was close to losing it all, I kept saying, 'this isn't the end.'

I still believe."

Carlson's Keys to Success

✓ Plan

All great leaders are able to execute, but to be successful you need to lay out your strategy.

✓ Team

Hire people to cover your weaknesses. If you're not an accountant or website designer, enlist people to help execute your plan.

✓ Persistence

If you hit a wall, push through it. The greatest rewards are getting past the most difficult situations.

✓ Passion

You won't be able to overcome obstacles in your business plan if you don't have a passion for the product.

Believe in what you're doing and you can overcome anything.

Serendipity

Chris Ye
CEO and Co-Founder of Uken Games

Ser-en-dip-i-ty, *noun. pl.* ser-in-dip-i-ties; 1. the act of finding something good or useful while not specifically searching for it. 2. good fortune; luck.

Award winning entrepreneur Chris Ye of Uken Games believes serendipity makes a good partner with business. It's played a major in his entrepreneurial career and he can pinpoint with laser precision the moments in his life when serendipity came calling.

"My family moved around a lot when I was young and I switched schools four times. In sixth grade I met my best friend, Ron, and he transformed my life. It was serendipitous. He was different, highly ambitious, and taught me about Bill Gates and Warren Buffet. We started the Stock Market Club and ran it together throughout high school. We organized virtual stock market competitions where you'd get a million bucks of fake money to invest in real companies, and then watch to see how you did within three to six months. It had a big impact, motivating me to follow companies and read the news.

"In my final year of high school, I watched Google's IPO and it also made a huge impression on me. I was blown away by how different the company was in terms of its attitude towards business and the investors. They weren't afraid to make big bets on long-term opportunities and they made it clear they wouldn't let short-term expectations drive decisions. That's when I started getting interested in technology companies."

While studying business at university, he went to several job fairs and found employment at Nortel for the next two summers, working in their accounting department.

"We occupied a massive campus and it was more than half empty. It was obvious Nortel's business was not going well and I started to think outside the box."

Ye joined Facebook as a user in 2005 and watched with interest when they began raising venture capital.

"I was too young to pay any meaningful attention during the first dotcom bubble, so I was fascinated when the Web 2.0 trend emerged. Photo and video sharing sites like Flickr, You Tube, and social networks like Myspace seemed to come from nowhere and overnight had millions of users. Then Facebook turned down a billion dollar buyout offer from Yahoo. It confirmed we were in a new era and that billion dollar businesses could be built by people who had the audacity to pursue an independent vision."

In his third year of university, Chris and a friend started a note-sharing website called NotesHQ. Using money they saved from summer jobs, they each put in twenty thousand dollars and then enrolled in the school of hard knocks. Their initial rollout attracted only a few hundred users, and their programming costs started to skyrocket when the site developed problems.

"For the most part, it was an expensive learning lesson," Chris admits. "Looking back, we did almost everything wrong and we didn't execute well."

Serendipity was about to come calling again, this time in the form of technology. Apple was launching its highly publicized smartphone and Chris was determined to get one.

"The first iPhone was released in 2007. It was only offered in the U.S. and quickly sold out everywhere. I finally bought one for one thousand dollars on eBay even though it retailed for only seven hundred. I didn't have much money at the time but I knew I had to own one. When it arrived, it felt like Christmas morning. As I held the device in my hand, I immediately thought, 'This is the future.' There were all sorts of interesting features but there was nothing as transformative as having the web in your pocket. I knew it was about to change the world."

Throughout university, Chris continued exploring his passion for technology and entrepreneurship by attending local tech conferences and meetups.

"Despite burning through most of my savings with my first business venture, I was quite hungry to try again. I went to the first Facebook development camp in Toronto. They had recently launched an initiative to allow third-party developers to build applications on their platform, and the camp was intended to get developers excited. They offered instant access to the eighty million users already on Facebook, an opportunity impossible to achieve while building a standalone website. It was quite a compelling opportunity."

Serendipity was knocking on Ye's door again.

"I walked around and introduced myself to several people and then I met Mark Lampert. We clicked right away and we immediately started talking about what we wanted to do with this Facebook platform."

Within two weeks, Lampert built a simple gifting application for Facebook to tie-in with the approach of Halloween. Named Twisted Trick or Treating, users visited each other's virtual houses and requested a gift. It was an immediate hit, reaching close to a million users.

"Mark was originally monetizing the app through standard banner ads, however, I thought we should tie in big brand names. I sent a proposal to every consumer branded company out there and Nestlé quickly came onboard. People were gifting virtual Smarties, Kit Kats, and Aeros. Throughout Halloween and Christmas there were hundreds of thousands of Nestlé branded gifts sent around the world and we made twenty thousand dollars."

Ye graduated from university in 2008, and when a corporate job opportunity fell through due to the economic recession he considered his options. Chris still had the entrepreneurial itch and teamed with Mark to learn how to code and design games. Working out of Mark's home, Superheroes Alliance was launched within four months and Uken Games was born.

"We made fourteen dollars our first day," Chris says laughing. "The game was free to play, but we sold virtual items to people who wanted a premium experience and the opportunity to move up more levels in the game. It gained momentum and within three months we had over fifty thousand users. By the end of the year, we were doing one thousand dollars a day in revenue. We had never built anything that large before and we were excited."

The Toronto Tech community had grown measurably in a few short months. Serendipity appeared again, when Ye and Lampert met Farham Thawar and Amar Varma who were running a business incubator called Extreme University. The two businessmen encouraged them to apply and, once accepted, Uken moved into a shared startup space. Being surrounded by other technology companies motivated the young entrepreneurs. They also started working closely with Varma and were able to raise another round of financing to fuel growth.

"We started out with a single game, then built an engine off the original code and launched six additional role-playing games. We also developed the concept of playing across multiple platforms very early. A person could start a game on the bus coming from work and re-launch the game on Facebook from their home computer, playing from the same account in a seamless fashion. We were one of the first companies to develop the concept and it was a big selling point. People who played across multiple platforms were three times more likely to engage with our game and spend money."

Uken Games was profitable right out of the gate and is now a multi-million dollar company employing sixty people with twenty million installed users.

"Mark and I have built a fantastic partnership and have been through a lot together. We think differently but we have a tremendous mutual respect for one another. We're very honest and we know what our strengths are. We've built an organization we are very proud of, with a lot of potential to move forward. We feel it has a great future."

Their journey hasn't always been perfect. Ye admits they've made many mistakes, lost several opportunities, and watched other companies grow faster.

"There were times we came very close to running out of cash. At one point, we made several key hires but weren't growing revenue fast enough. It was a scary time, but we pulled through it by keeping our expenses low and lean."

The smartphone dramatically changed the world and people are waiting eagerly to see what new technology is emerging. Ye confirms the pioneering stage is over and the industry is in its growth phase.

"It's an exhilarating time to be an entrepreneur because all the things around us are becoming smart devices. I believe we'll make big strides in the next five years and I'm excited about the future. As those technologies emerge there will be opportunities to build around them.

"A lot of people fear change, but to me it spells opportunity. It means life is getting better, faster, and more efficient and it's incredibly positive for the world. Aspiring entrepreneurs need to be thoughtful about the future and get involved in things they are passionate about. Passion will carry you through the rollercoaster ride of business and while success isn't guaranteed, you'll learn and grow as a person.

"Put yourself out there and don't be afraid of serendipity. Be open to it. I met my friend, Ron, in elementary school and he motivated me. I saw a glimpse of the future when I held the first iPhone in my hands. I found Mark and we clicked right away, then went on to found Uken Games. All those serendipitous moments had an immense impact on my life and they all happened out of the blue.

"At Uken, I spend my day collaborating with talented and passionate people who care about our vision: delivering fun to the world. We're fortunate to be in a position where there are many opportunities and our business is growing. Above all, we just love what we do."

That's serendipity.

Eight Lessons I've Learned, by Chris Ye

✓ It's not a sprint, it's a marathon. Plan for the long term and be focused.

✓ Define a clear vision and be its story teller.

✓ Keep it lean. You're always going to be short on resources, money, talent, ideas, or time. Be thoughtful about where you spend them.

✓ Question everything. Never be afraid to ask why.

✓ People are everything. They are more important than any product you're building or whether you're hitting your financial goals. People will define the future of your company.

Shake Things Up a Bit

Manjit and Ravinder Minhas
Minhas Creek Craft Brewing Co.

Manjit Minhas' lemonade stand in Calgary had a revolving sign. The ten year old entrepreneur and her little brother Ravinder would charge the kids in their neighbourhood twenty-five cents a cup, however, when an adult approached, their sign switched to fifty cents.

"My mom wasn't impressed," Manjit laughs, "but we thought we were really smart."

They are a family of entrepreneurs and aren't afraid of taking risks in the business world. When their father was given a severance package from his oil company, he was intrigued by the news Alberta was privatizing the sale of alcohol. He and his wife cobbled together their savings, opened OK Liquor Store in Calgary, and everyone was put to work making sure it was successful right from the start.

"Weekends, holidays, and Christmas, we always worked at the store," Manjit recalls. "We would bag, organize the stock room; we did anything Mom and Dad wanted us to do."

They also were extremely competitive with each other. When their parents expanded their operation, the brother and sister split up to work at different locations.

"We had a competition," Ravinder says. "We'd pick a brand and compete to see how many cases we could sell. What it taught us was the power of the retailer and the knowledge provided to the consumer. We knew the product inside and out and what customers wanted to buy."

They were also watching market trends and the top brands selling for premium prices. The enterprising siblings had an idea for their parents, suggesting they create a house brand and sell top quality liquor at a low price.

"We came up with a line of spirits: rum, rye, brandy, scotch, and tequila. We labeled it OK Liquor and soon we were getting calls from others wanting to sell the product. Eventually our line was being sold in 1,200 stores."

As Ravinder looks back on those early days he's shocked they did so well. "We had the ugliest label in the world but it was extremely successful. It confirmed our theory that if we put out a high quality product, no matter what the bottle looked like, it would catch the attention of the consumer."

By now, Manjit and Ravinder were in university and decided it was time to go into the beer industry.

"We felt there was no competition," she recalls. "They were selling inferior beer in Alberta, not only to students but to other people who drank beer. It was ridiculous."

The Minhases took their business plan to the bank and asked for a loan. Both were under the age of twenty at the time so the bank was only going to give them the money if their parents co-signed the paperwork. Determined to do it on their own, they left the bank and Manjit sold her SUV for ten thousand dollars.

"That became our seed money," Ravinder says proudly. "We asked our suppliers for terms over ninety days and promised the product would be sold right away."

The suppliers agreed and the siblings went to work. They came up with a Buck a Beer marketing strategy and called it Mountain Crest Lager.

"We did gorilla marketing, anything we could do for cheap," Manjit recalls, smiling as she recalls the early days. "We did You Tube videos instead of commercials, we contacted the media and PR agencies. We conducted tastings everywhere and did what we could to get the brand in people's faces, but it was also a great product and it had legs of its own."

As beer sales began to soar, they recognized the bank had done them a favour by not granting them a loan.

"We realized we could work with lower overheads if we didn't have expenses," Ravinder explains. "We didn't have to please any shareholders, so our focus was one hundred percent on our business. It became our staple to work with less, but to be quicker in the market and to make do."

It wasn't long before they began creating products for every category, and sales went through the roof. They were so successful, they put in an offer to buy an existing brew company in Wisconsin, and when the deal was done they had become the youngest brewery owners in the world.

Ravinder goes back to the night the deal became final. "It was around midnight and walking down to the production floor, I thought, 'Wow, we own this!' It was surreal. I ran back upstairs and grabbed my sister. We went outside and we said, 'This is ours!'"

Manjit was twenty-four years old and Ravinder was twenty-two.

"It's interesting because I don't think of myself as the youngest of anything," Manjit tells me from her office in Calgary. "Our industry has been around for a long time so it's refreshing to know someone new can come in, be successful, and shake things up a bit."

Ten years later the siblings are still working together growing the brand and expanding into new markets.

"We're still partners today and it's lots of fun," Manjit says. "As siblings, it's good to have family around, that's for sure. It's nice to share the joys with each other and have someone to lean on."

"She brings calmness and execution to our company," Ravinder adds. "I bring the dreams and keep everyone thinking big."

The Minhases have done it on their own without bringing in partners, loans, or investors. They started with zero debt and have grown internally by reinvesting profits. Their growth curve as entrepreneurs has been swift, however, Manjit admits there have been failures along the way.

"No one is successful the first time around. Most people aren't. It takes perseverance and hard work. If success was easy everyone would have it.

When you see success stories, don't think it happened overnight."

She believes there are several key strategies people starting their own business should adhere to.

"You have to believe in your product and have passion for what you do. Set goals for yourself. I still have monthly and yearly goals, personally and for the company. Whether you reach them or not, the point is, you are still working towards them. With that, you create a vision for yourself and your company. It takes guts and vision to develop what you stand for. Wake up in the morning and be driven to get where you are going."

Manjit's voice grows firmer when she says it's important to never compromise your values or your financial well-being to propel a company forward.

"Stay within your means," she suggests strongly. "Some go big right away but that sometimes comes with a high cost that you can't pay back. It's important you live and spend what you have been given. Keep a tight pocket in the beginning as expenses can go out of control and make or break you."

Ravinder is also passionate about what it takes to become successful in today's marketplace. "There are a million reasons why you might fail," he tells me, "but there are three reasons why you're going to succeed. They are strong salesmanship, high quality products, and low prices."

"If necessary, don't be afraid to hire outside companies to refocus," Manjit adds. "It's remarkable how a little tweaking in a product or service can make the difference during the tough times."

She points to a time in the evolution of their beer when they needed to listen to the consumer.

"Early on, we thought we'd sell a strong beer at a great price. We were going to be close to 6% alcohol and everyone else was 5%. We listened to people who said it was too strong so we brought it down to 5.5%. We kept it there and Mountain Crest became our flagship brand. We listened, tweaked it, and the beer ended up a winner."

The award winning siblings appear to have it all, however, their success has come with a price.

"There are many things people haven't seen." Manjit adds. "At university, we were not always at the parties. We were working late nights and eating, sleeping, and breathing our company. It's been tough and not as glamorous as people think."

"I don't regret it," Ravinder says. "It was an exciting time. The fun we have now has more than made up for our sacrifices. We kept reminding each other there would be an opportunity in life where we would have so much more – if we could just get through the pain of the early days."

Now that's turning the lemons of business into brewery gold.

Brewing up Excellence

✓ Believe in your product and have passion for what you do.

✓ Set your goals. They will provide a vision for yourself and the company.

✓ Keep a tight pocket in the beginning because expenses can go out of control and make or break you. It's important to keep a close eye on overhead.

✓ There is no substitute for hard work. Success is not built overnight, it takes lots of hard work and perseverance.

✓ Your product or service should be flexible for what the market is calling for. Hire outside companies to refocus. It's remarkable how a little bit of tweaking in product or service can make a difference in the tough times.

Learn to Work Together

Patricia Turner
President and CEO of E.T. Developments Ltd.

"We need to walk side-by-side and learn to work together to build a better future," Patricia Turner tells me from her construction office in Grand Rapids, Manitoba. She is on a mission to not only make life better for First Nations people, but for everyone in Canada. Inspirational, strong, and opinionated, Turner is a trailblazer and her pioneering spirit and visionary leadership is a compelling tale of big-picture thinking and entrepreneurship.

Pat is the President and CEO of a successful construction company in northern Manitoba. Over the years, she has been a First Nations chief, a government advisor, and federal employment officer. She's come a long way from counting dimes, nickels, and pennies on the floor of a canteen in a residential school in Dauphin, Manitoba.

"My dad went to Kelsey in northern Manitoba to work on the new hydro generation station, so at four-and-a-half years old, I was sent to Dauphin."

The administrator didn't know what to do with the young child who was too young to start school. Working in the canteen, he asked Pat to separate the coins and put them into neat rolls.

"He taught me how to count and save money. I became smart with numbers and it stayed with me my whole life."

The enterprising pre-schooler found another job when an older boy asked her to deliver a note to a girl in an upstairs classroom.

"I charged him a dime and soon I was delivering lots of notes. I was running a courier service without realizing it," Pat says with a laugh. "In order to get independence, I realized you needed money and security to carry you forward in life."

Returning to the reserve when she was fifteen, she held a series of odd jobs including reading letters in English for the chief and council members. She met a young construction worker named Herman, married, and then became a mother, giving birth to two boys and a girl, all a year apart. While raising her family, Pat always found time to read. History and science books were her favorite and she spent hours learning about life in the middle ages and the pioneers who had come to North America.

"When my youngest enrolled in kindergarten, I went back to school too. I earned my grade twelve and found a job working for the band administrator. I transferred over to project manager when they were building a new office and a store. That's when I fell in love with construction. I made sure the money was in place and the workers were getting paid. We had a ribbon-cutting ceremony with the chief and council. I felt proud I had helped build something."

Turner stayed on with the tribal council working as a local government advisor. She helped the First Nations administration with their books, managing property, and new projects. Applying to the federal government, she became an employment officer then transferred to Indian Affairs a year later. She loved her job, however, she had to leave her husband behind in Grand Rapids while she traveled with the children and worked throughout Manitoba.

"My husband spent weekends with us and we made it work. It was a juggling act, but I always found I liked challenges in my life because it made me stronger. It was challenging for my husband too."

After a series of cutbacks at the federal level, Pat was offered a retirement package and, at the age of thirty-eight, she took it. Moving back to Grand Rapids, it didn't take long to find her next challenge. She ran for the position of chief and served for a term as head of her band.

"I found politics were not for me. As a leader, you have to work with the government of the day and whoever is in power. I'm a do-er, so I was frustrated when I couldn't get things done quickly."

Two key events in Turner's life were about to merge. Herman had been running a small construction company and Pat decided to join the family business. "I thought, 'What the heck. I like construction and it's a natural fit for both of us.'" She also learned an outside company had been brought onto the reserve to put in water and sewer lines.

"I went to see the foreman every day because I knew he needed help," Pat recalls, "and finally he told me, 'If you can get a bigger loader and a semi-trailer truck, then you will have a job for the next two years.' Two big banks turned me down, saying I didn't have a full-time job and we didn't have the money to back us up. I went to a credit union and showed them my proposal. I waited for fifteen minutes and I was sweating. Then the banker walked over to me and said, 'Pat, we have decided to give you the money.' I hugged him and almost cried. I said, 'If I don't pay you back, I promise to drive the loader right to your doorstep.' We all laughed. Then the banker told me I had a lot of guts and he knew I was honest. We bought the equipment."

By this time, Pat's children had grown and moved out so she turned a bedroom into an office and began managing their new enterprise from home. Putting together a one-page description of their company, she started marketing their services of construction, building roads, and installing water and sewer lines.

"We even hauled lumber and did snow removal," Pat says with pride. "I went to the First Nations and they were supportive, but I knew we'd have to step out of the box to be successful. I went to Manitoba Hydro and local businesses, and we got work."

E.T. Developments began to grow under Pat's leadership and they put all their profits back into expanding the company.

"Every year we bought a bigger excavator and added more tractor-trailers. We bought more tandems and dozers then moved to the edge of the reserve and built a big five thousand square foot shop. We never touched one penny of the profits and all the money we had went into paying for the building. We couldn't afford holidays and we didn't go out for dinner."

The hard work and sacrifice paid off. Today, they have twenty-nine employees and have become a success story. They have even started a sideline business called Triple T Cabins and rent rooms out to construction crews.

"It's challenging to be a woman in the construction industry," Pat admits. "When I first started, I had to work twice as hard as the men. I stood ten feet tall the day I was accepted in business and fit in. We've all taken a big step forward and have gone through doors that were never open to us.

"It's also important people realize First Nation businesses are a big part of the economy today. My dream is to have an Aboriginal Chamber of Commerce set up in every province in Canada. Our business people need to get into the system so we can help this country and population by continuing to contribute and pay taxes. Then we won't be so reliant on welfare and other social systems. The First Nations doesn't own my business, I do. Aboriginal people are successful in their own right and they should be acknowledged."

As a respected and valued businessperson within her community and in Canada, Pat Turner has this to say to aspiring entrepreneurs.

"Be the best you can be and do it as honestly as you can. You have to expand and grow with the business. Sell it to the people and find out who you are catering to. Today, we have the internet and emails but I find it's good to talk to people face-to-face and promote your business."

Pat prefers to lead by example, and is inspiring the next generation of women construction workers in her own humble way.

"I see women running trucks on the road and I watch them on the jobs. I feel very proud and think to myself, 'I wonder if they know I was part of the pioneer group?' They probably think I'm a secretary, but that's not important to me. I just smile and go back to work."

For all of us, that's the best advice of all.

Patricia's Points

✓ Be honest about your company and the products you sell.

✓ If you can't manage your money then find someone to manage it for you.

✓ It's all about teamwork. There is no such thing as *I*.

✓ Identify the strengths in your employees and supervisors. Discover their hidden talents and let them do what they do best.

✓ Learn to work together. Support other businesses and they in turn will help you. It doesn't matter if there are ten businesses in a group. At the end of the day we'll all be counting our money.

Partnering Successfully _____

Ricardo and Gloria Roheim McRae
Co-Founders of Wedge15

"I now pronounce you entrepreneur and entrepreneur."

Cue the organ and grab the confetti as they walk down the aisle into a life of wedded business bliss. People all over the world have asked the question; can a man and woman successfully run a company together and still maintain a strong marriage? For Ricardo McRae and Gloria Roheim McRae, the answer is a resounding yes!

"We put our marriage first," Gloria says. "We make sure our married life has the integrity and the communication it requires to deal with any upsets. We believe in work-life integration rather than balance. Our business is directly integrated into our personal life."

Ricardo agrees. "Working together intensifies your relationship and commitment to each other. I feel it brings us closer."

It's all sounding a little too perfect so I ask the big question; do they ever fight?

"Oh my God, yes," laughs Gloria, "however, we know there's way more at stake. We realized letting situations go on for a long time was detrimental to our business so we needed to learn to handle our disagreements amicably."

"You must give the other person the grace to be human," Ricardo says. "It's very important."

The dynamic couple own Wedge15, a digital strategy and branding company. They met through a mutual acquaintance and clicked immediately even though there was a fifteen year age difference.

"Our friend invited us both for coffee but she never showed up," Ricardo says, smiling at the memory. "Gloria and I met and our coffee break turned into an eight hour meeting. We talked about everything in the world, shutting down the Starbucks and then an Indian restaurant nearby."

"We had so much in common," Gloria says. "We had a real heart-to-heart talk; it was intense and very inspiring. I realized we had so much in common. A month later we went on our first official date and committed to each other that night."

The two entrepreneurs seemed ordained to meet, however, each took a different path to get to the coffee shop of destiny. Ricardo was born in Guyana and immigrated to Canada to be with his dad when he was seventeen. His first business was a runaway hit. Needing money for school, he started RHR Student Painters. After writing an article for the local paper about his new venture, his business exploded when the phone started ringing off the hook. At the age of eighteen, Ricardo was managing sixteen employees and the budding entrepreneur mastered his first lesson.

"I learned to take charge instead of waiting for someone else to do it for me," McRae says.

Gloria Roheim says she wasn't the child with the corner lemonade stand, however she was an international globe trotter by the age of five.

"My parents divorced and my father moved back to Europe," Gloria says, "so I spent one year in Hungary with him and the following year in Toronto with my mother. Going back and forth between the two countries taught me how to navigate throughout the world and to constantly be flexible."

Graduating from university after studying art and business, Ricardo "went where the work was" and became a project manager for a tech company before moving on to account sales for telecommunications giant Worldcom. McRae was working hard and making good money, then a tragic event changed his life and career forever.

"My best friend was diagnosed with terminal cancer," Ricardo says sadly. "Before he died, he told me his biggest regret in life was not finishing his jazz album so his son could hear him play music. Someone I loved and respected was going to his grave not having achieved what he was meant to do. I didn't want it to happen to me so I resigned from my job at Worldcom and became an artist."

McRae found a studio in downtown Toronto above a Chinese food restaurant. Painting and drawing, Ricardo says he was able to sell his work, but it wasn't enough to make a decent living. Was there a way to combine his artistic side with business?

"People kept asking me to build websites and I found it to be an interesting combination of business and art. I loved the designing, building, and the colours. It seemed to blend everything I learned in my life. I called my new company the Ricardo McRae Agency and offered branding, design, and social media to help companies get an advantage over their competition."

As Ricardo was building his business, Gloria entered the workforce. She powered her way through high school, graduating early, and then obtained a degree at McGill before getting her Master's at the University of Toronto.

"I worked full-time at a bank while going to school and came out debt free. I worked for the provincial Minister of Finance as a policy advisor and then went into project management for a non-profit organization. During vacations, I took on special projects in Montenegro and Kosovo doing field work. I was always resourceful at making things work."

Gloria was also very adept at social media, writing a popular blog. She knew about market reach and all the elements lending themselves to being effective online.

"I was the generation with Facebook, Twitter, and had been blogging for years. I decided traditional employment was not for me and it was time to begin my own business. I started a social media agency offering my services and training."

With a twist of fate from the universe and a well-meaning friend who saw the magic of a possible union, Ricardo and Gloria went out for their memorable coffee. Their businesses were flourishing along with their new relationship, and soon both began to intersect.

"We started bidding on the same jobs," Gloria says. "I had been subcontracting work to Ricardo for websites and branding, and in many cases we noticed we made more money when we collaborated."

Deciding to merge their companies, they were launched into a world of legal documents and tough questions about life and death. Ricardo tells me they hired a lawyer.

"There were shareholders agreements to put together. We had to ask ourselves, 'What happens if one of us loses our faculties? What about divorce?' Getting real on those discussions was very sobering. We had to plan it all out in advance and we thought about every aspect deeply. Should something happen, we have a clause the other person has the first option to buy the other out, and there is only one opportunity to accept or decline. No back and forth."

With their partnership contract signed and their wedding scheduled to take place two months later, Gloria and Ricardo faced a moment of crisis, testing their relationship and business.

"We won a bid to produce a documentary," explains Gloria. "It was a film on the fashion industry in Trinidad and Tobago. We were working with a foreign government on a timeline and a huge six-figure contract, but the payments weren't coming through. We had to raise capital in twenty-four hours, play the political games to safeguard the contract, and in the middle of it all Ricardo's back went out. We were in over our head, without the proper legal and financial advisors to take on a project of this nature. We pulled through it because that's how we roll. We obtained the money, finished the film, and launched it to great success. It solidified our partnership and our impending marriage."

"It was a massive moment for us as partners and as a couple," Ricardo adds. "We saw each other's character under pressure. It was a testament to our relationship."

I ask the McRae's to share the other techniques they've learned to run a successful business and still keep their marriage intact. They grow thoughtful, then agree unanimously on one key factor, communication.

"You can't tell each other what to do," Gloria says. "I learned the way I communicate doesn't work for Ricardo. What I thought was direct conversation sounded like a command to him. In any work environment or business it's more fragile when dealing with a spouse. What seems like an obvious communication to you can land in all the wrong ways to the other person, especially when you're in an intimate relationship.

"We also had to work on how we approach business. I'm the early bird, quick and right to the punch. Ricardo has a different style; he waits and watches until he feels it's time to act. We both achieve success, but where I feel he's moving slowly, he thinks I'm rushing. We've learned to be mindful of each other because you have a lot more at stake if you're ignoring the warning signs and working with your partner.

"We had to learn only one of us can lead at a time. It doesn't work with both of us trying to be the leader in the conversation or meeting. It becomes a competition to be heard instead of a collaborative team approach to doing business."

I ask Ricardo how important boundaries are to running a company with your spouse. Do they talk about business day and night?

"Shutting the computers off at 6 p.m. doesn't work for us," he says. "We get frustrated. We make sure to schedule a date-night every week and go out for dinner. We also work out together and go away for weekends. Most of the time we do talk about business, but it's okay because it's driving our passion and it's hard to shut off what we love."

"I believe, at the end of the day, if you don't believe you're here for a bigger purpose and only working for a living, then being an entrepreneur is not for you," Gloria says candidly. "You must grow as a businessperson and the reward is the people you meet along the way who make your life much more fulfilling."

The bottom line for this power couple?

"Our relationship comes before our business together," says Ricardo. "It's written in our contract too. Being an entrepreneur is the most challenging, rewarding, frustrating, beautiful thing you will ever take on in your life. There's no school for becoming an entrepreneur but there's nothing like it in the world. It's comparable to sailing a ship, testing the water, and changing course."

The McRae's pause and look at each other, smiling in agreement. "We love it."

The McRae Guide to Partnering Successfully

✓ Develop a shared vision, and take the time to align your goals.

✓ Replace the pursuit of work-life *balance* with work-life *integration*.

✓ Openly discuss your hot buttons, and agree on how best to support the other.

✓ Debrief, debrief, debrief. Regular communication makes all the difference.

✓ Play to your strengths. Create opportunities for your partner to shine.

Be Passionate About Success

Surjit Babra
Founder and Chairman/CEO
SkyLink Group

"I am a serial entrepreneur."

Surjit Babra has come a long way from working on a machine shop floor in an auto parts company to owning multiple businesses in the travel and aviation industry. What drives this highly successful businessman?

"Passion," he tells me strongly. "I am passionate about success. Every day I worked at the auto parts company I said to myself, 'This is not what I want.' I hated it." Babra pauses for a moment, and then roars with laughter as he says, "I hated it with a passion!

"I had to get out of it so I began working at a travel agency as an intern. Instead of teaching me business, my boss had me get coffee every time a customer came into the shop. That is when I decided I wanted to be a boss. I come from an immigrant family and we started with nothing. Zero is very a very powerful number and the only way to go is up. Remember, if you have nothing you can't fail."

While he stood around waiting to get coffee for everyone in the travel agency, Surjit opened his eyes and ears, learning everything he could about the business.

"I had no money but I had sheer passion and the drive to be successful. I decided to invest in myself. I was my own economic power."

Graduating from fetching coffee to issuing and delivering tickets, it wasn't long before Babra took on a partner and opened his own travel agency. It was a small office and only big enough for two desks.

"It was a cold day in London and I saw ray of sunshine go across my desk. I called my new company Sunbeam Travel."

Babra's plan was to expand quickly and efficiently. All the profits of the company were put back into the business and soon he had fourteen offices throughout Europe. When it was time to expand again, Surjit traveled to North America.

"We were sending tourists to Canada so I decided to open an office in Toronto. I hit a big hurdle when I went in front of FIRA, the Foreign Investment Review Agency. They told me I wasn't going to be hiring enough Canadians for my application to be approved. So I said to the agent, "One day I will hire six hundred Canadians. Right now, I only want one office so my clients can be taken care of."

Babra was granted permission to go into business in Canada.

"I opened my agency on King Street in Toronto and within three months I hired an employee. Sunbeam was the holding company and was publicly traded as SkyLink."

The year was 1979, and Babra didn't count on the economy turning on him. Within a few months, a crippling recession took hold of the country.

"The first year was tough. It wasn't long before I moved to New York and then opened agencies in Chicago, Los Angeles, and Las Vegas. I kept costs tight and put in long hours of work. Once one was successful, I moved onto the next city. My parents had taught me to keep my costs low. There's a saying, 'Cut your cloth according to your size.' I was drawing twenty-five percent less salary than my lowest paid employees."

After nine years of expansion in the U.S., Babra took on a partner and moved back to Toronto to start a new head office.

"Bankers don't want to give you financing if you don't have money. I had to use my own capital. I called it *sweat equity*. You have your brains and your sweat. Even when I married and started a family I plowed a lot of the profits back into the company. The apartments we lived in may have been small but I always made sure my family was taken care of."

As Surjit built the company, he allowed himself one important expenditure. He bought books, read voraciously, and went to self-improvement courses.

"To dream big is nice, however, you must invest in yourself. The first book I read was Dale Carnegie's, *How to Win Friends and Influence People*. It impacted me in a big way. Today, I buy lots of copies and give them to people for free."

Babra and SkyLink seemed to be on an upwards trajectory towards major success. Then the morning of September 11, 2001, arrived. As he watched the airplanes crash into the World Trade Centre he saw his business explode into a sea of red.

"9/11 was the worst period in my life. We had to refund everyone's tickets and people were bouncing cheques. The whole industry suffered. Many of my employees saw the trouble I was in and offered to work for free. I told them, 'No, you're getting paid. Thank you, but don't even think about it.' It's all about the University of Hard Knocks and sometimes there is nothing you can do about it."

Babra and SkyLink weathered the storm and fallout from the terrorist attacks. Surjit says he put his faith in a higher power.

"I have an insurance policy and it's simple. I do the best I can and a little bit more, then leave the rest to God. I believe it's His world and He'll take care of me."

As people regained their confidence in the travel industry and found the courage to board airplanes again, Babra took his brand to the next level. By 2008, he owned multiple travel and aviation companies employing twelve hundred people around the world. When you're riding a wave of success, other people start to take notice.

"None of my companies were for sale. Still, they came to me wanting to acquire one of the divisions called SkyLink Aviation. I agreed, and sold it for 125 million to a private equity fund. The sale process was painful and frustrating but I remained focused with the end goal in mind. Two years later, another private equity fund inquired about SkyLink Travel, however, they wanted me to stay on as CEO. Sitting down, I wrote out the pros and cons of the deal. I asked myself, 'Gain or pain?' The pain would be letting my baby go and letting other people take part in the day-to-day decision making. I knew it wasn't going to be easy working with private equity funds and bean counters. Then I thought about gain. Cash in the bank is good, right? I'd have the money to grow other businesses and to take them to the next step. So I sold, and have joined a bigger team with more arms and hands to grow the travel business and ride the next wave of travel."

With the 400 million dollar deal completed, Babra began building the next phase of his empire.

"I have multiple companies and I do the strategic planning. It's different than owning a company and being the CEO. I service my staff and managers as if they are my customers and bosses, developing strategy for them and, in turn, they produce income for me."

Babra's leadership and strategic thinking has served the group of companies well. In 2012, he won the Queen's Diamond Jubilee Award and was the only Canadian to be honoured with a prestigious World Travel Award.

Surjit is often asked for advice and speaks to business students, sharing his thoughts on success and what it takes to become an entrepreneur.

"I ask students, 'Did you stop and think?' Most people never take any time-outs. They only work, and soon months and years have passed. Stop often. Think, plan, and focus."

Babra is fond of telling the story about the man who was cutting a log with a blunt saw. "Someone asked, 'Why don't you sharpen your saw? It will make the job easier.' The man replied, 'I don't have time and I can't stop.' It took him five hours to finish the job."

Babra stops to ponder the story, then says, "He could have cut the log in half the time had he stopped a moment and sharpened his blade. Hard work is good but be smart about it.

"I also believe in auto-suggestion. Talk to yourself all the time. Call yourself a king, then you will become one. People are their worst enemy. The world doesn't put you down. You do. Think positive. Get up in the morning and say,

'Wow, what a great day,' and you'll have one."

Surjit also believes in helping others. He's won numerous business awards, however, he's the most proud of the work he's doing with SkyLink Children's Charity. In 2005, Babra received the Mother Teresa Humanitarian Award in Los Angeles. A year later, he and his partner Walter Arbib received the B'nai Brith Award of Merit honoring their charitable work around the globe. It was the first time in their 130 year history that B'nai Brith honoured someone not of Jewish descent. Shyamala Cowsik, who was the High Commissioner for India at the time, attended the event. As she presented Surjit with another award, the prestigious Robe of Honour, Cowsik said, "Mr. Babra is a gift from his motherland India to Canada, his adopted homeland."

Over the years, SkyLink has assisted in bringing troops, trucks, and medical supplics to countries ravaged by earthquakes and war. They've been in Iraq and Afghanistan, and carried Canadian DART troops to Sri Lanka to help with tsunami relief work. They've flown medicine, personnel, and equipment around the world to help with numerous natural disasters, and have generously helped in Canada during the Manitoba floods and the Quebec ice storm.

"For me, I will have achieved success if I leave the world a better place than when I entered it. If people tell me they have no money to help others, I ask they give their time. Or I say, 'Can you pray for the man in Somalia who is hungry?' If they say yes, then I tell them, 'Okay, now you're giving.'

"Every person has a right to make it in this world. Life is not fair and the only thing equal is time. You have twenty-four hours every day just like everyone else. Now go out and use it!"

Babra's Business Bites

✓ Dream big.

✓ Make written plans and update them often.

✓ Invest in yourself. Focus on your abilities and improve on them.

✓ Surround yourself with quality people who energize you.

✓ Stay on track. When a bad bump comes along, many people change course too quickly. Have a well thought out plan and stick to it.

Research and Be Disciplined

Pierre Ferland
Caribbean Entrepreneur
Pineapple Pete Restaurant and Bar

Pierre Ferland walks through his busy restaurant on the Caribbean island of St. Maarten, smiling and talking to customers in English and French. His easy smile and French accent give him a charismatic charm that is hard to ignore. He waves to the police chief settling in for lunch, shakes the hands of some returning tourists, and then stops to assist a busy waiter.

Born on a farm outside of Quebec City, Pierre and his ten brothers and sisters learned the importance of working hard. At the age of nine, Pierre decided to go into the worm harvesting business. His uncle ran a trout farm up the road and the going rate for worms was fifteen cents. Finding a piece of scrap wood, Ferland designed a hand painted sign offering his crawlers for five cents.

"When I was eleven, I made fifteen hundred bucks but then catastrophe struck when I ran out of worms. So I purchased more for fifteen cents but kept my selling price at a nickel. Even then I knew how important it was not to lose a customer."

Ferland excelled at school and received good grades yet he knew a post-secondary education would only happen if he put himself through university. With the savings from his worm business in the bank, he went to work at a local restaurant chain and began acquiring the money he'd need for schooling.

"I was very shy, with zero experience and no people skills, so they put me as a dishwasher. That lasted fifteen minutes. They said I was too quick and showed me the kitchen. I moved along very fast, becoming assistant manager of forty-five people in just over a year."

Pierre excelled in the restaurant business and learned a valuable lesson about managing people. "You can't command respect," he says firmly, "you have to earn it."

Pursuing a civil engineering degree, Ferland and a friend set off on a road trip to the west coast. Growing up in Quebec meant they were fluent in French, so Pierre's goal was to explore the country and learn a second language.

"We had an English dictionary in the car. Every night we would do an exam. Whoever lost had to buy dinner." Ferland stops and then laughs as he adds, "My friend had to pay a lot.

"I started working at the Meridian Hotel in Vancouver which is the best one out there. I refused to learn from anyone else. I wanted to see what they do, how they do it, and learn time management. It was great experience."

His job was rewarding but exhausting. After working grueling eighty hour weeks, Ferland jumped at the chance to take a holiday when a friend invited him to visit Hawaii. The vacation proved to be a turning point when he discovered two things he loved.

"There were a lot of pineapples in Hawaii," Pierre says chuckling, "and I also discovered I liked the warm weather better than the cold in Canada. Fortunately, I had a contact in the Cayman Islands who told me the Westin was opening a new hotel. I cut my Hawaii trip short, contacted the hotel, and they offered me a job as a waiter."

Ferland packed up his belongings and moved to the Cayman Islands. With the hotel still in the final stages of construction, Pierre joined the other food service people and helped scrape floors and move furniture into place.

"They flew in a banquet director from New York. I went to the corporate director and told him I have a lot of experience and if they needed help I would be glad to lend a hand. Within a week, I became banquet manager and they sent the other guy back. In my second year, I became the maître d' of an exclusive French restaurant. It was a good job but I decided to explore the

Caribbean. When I landed in St. Maarten in 1996, I knew I was here to stay."

Ferland worked as a manager at a popular restaurant for three years, learning how business was done on the island. He struck out on his own, opening two restaurants, but each time they started to turn a profit, Pierre found himself frozen out.

"They took my third of the shares," he says honestly. "When you are trustworthy, you think you can trust others." Pierre grows silent, and then says with a shrug, "I learned a valuable lesson."

Undeterred, he struck out on his own, buying an existing steakhouse in Simpson Bay.

"The place was a mess. I had to re-do the dining room and the kitchen. While I was renovating, I opened a sports bar across the road, and named it Time Out. People told me I was crazy because there was a casino with free drinks next door but I did very well. I served sandwiches, hot dogs, and purchased two toaster ovens to make small pizzas. I sold forty-eight one night. It meant little sleep, but I put all the profit back into opening the main restaurant across the street."

The renovation wasn't going well. Hit with numerous problems and delays, his plan of closing for two weeks stretched to three months and Ferland's cash ran out.

"I put together a business plan and flew home to Quebec for two days to talk to my brother. I had never asked anyone for anything and I felt ashamed. I showed him my proposal for the restaurant and explained that I was out of money. He looked at me and said, 'You're my brother and I believe in you. I don't need your business plan.'"

With the loan in hand, Pierre returned to St. Maarten to finish the restaurant. When it came time to name his new venture he decided Pierre's didn't sound right. He wanted something friendly and casual. Three days later, Pineapple Pete was ready for business.

Focusing on quality food and service, Ferland began to market his restaurant to the neighbouring hotels.

"We held bingo games in the hotels and the prize was dinner for one, never for two. I knew the winner would come with a spouse. That way I would break even and make the place look busy. I also knew if they came to the restaurant once, they would be back again."

As he watched his restaurant become busier with each passing night, he had to withstand considerable negative feedback.

"People on the island gave me six months, or told me to shut down. They said I had a bad location, and no one had ever made it in the area because it was too far down Simpson Bay. I ignored them all. It was hard to work lunch and dinner and then cross over to the sports bar and close each night. Between Pineapple Pete and Time Out, I worked 120 hours a week for six straight months."

It paid off. Ferland's restaurant quickly became an island favourite and within a year and a half he was able to repay his brother.

"I began flying my family members to St. Maarten to come and enjoy a vacation. My brother would never accept, so I had to trick him into coming. I told him I was overwhelmed and needed help," Pierre recalls with a chuckle. "He walked into my restaurant, looked around and said, 'You did well.' It was such a proud moment for me because I found out later it was the first vacation he had taken in his life."

Pierre's eyes fill with tears as he recalls that emotional moment with his brother. Bowing his head and studying the desk for a moment, he reveals his father passed away too soon to see his island success but his mother often travels to St. Maarten to visit.

"My mom is so proud. She's proud of all her children," he tells me through his tears. She said, 'Remember your sports bar and how hard you worked with all those little pizzas? Now look what you have!'

"You need to be able to live away from your family and it gets to you," he tells me softly. Steeling himself, he says, "I miss my mom, brothers, and sisters but living far away you have to learn how to control being homesick. It still happens to me after twenty-two years, so I fly home a lot."

Ferland is smiling again, pointing out he doesn't have to shovel snow during a tough Canadian winter, although he admits conducting business in a tourist region has its challenges.

"It always looks nicer from the other side. Make sure you choose a business you have experience in, learn the market and the labour force. Study the government, their tax system, and how to get work permits.

"You have to stay away from the temptations of the islands like drinking, drugs, and gambling. It's self-discipline, period," Ferland says firmly. "It's the only thing that will get you through. Set an example for your staff because everyone relies on you. When I walk in, the restaurant runs better. You must bring your level of energy to the place."

Pineapple Pete opened in 2004. Today, Ferland owns five businesses with just under eighty staff members. He won employer of the year in 2008, restaurateur of the year in 2012, and the Canwest newspaper group named his dining establishment one of the ten best restaurants in the world. Pierre is proud but also humble when talking about his success.

"I've earned my stripes but I try to improve everyday. I also reward people who have grown with me. Think about cow manure," Ferland says with a grin as he leans into the desk to make a point. "If it falls in one pile everything under it dies. But if you spread it around, everybody grows!"

The boy that grew up on a farm learned well.

"Any manager that works with me will be taught everything in order to run their own business. I helped two of my chefs open restaurants. I was helped, so now I give back. It's a wheel."

The single father of two children, Ferland is showing them how important it is to reach out to other people. Pierre contributes money and resources to the island, supporting local churches, numerous charities, sports teams, musicians, and authors but he doesn't want any special recognition. "I didn't do it for publicity," he tells me earnestly, "I did it because I care and I can."

"My priorities have changed. I wanted a Pineapple Pete on every single Caribbean island. Now I just want to be a perfect dad. I make them lunch and pick them up from school. Wednesday nights, I cook dinner. I'm okay with my business the way it is right now and I don't have to expand until they are older."

With our interview coming to a close, Pierre is anxious to get back to work. He has to order five hundred pounds of lobster, talk to his staff, deliver a lunch to a customer, and help a new waiter. He's at the beginning of what will be a fourteen hour day, but Pierre Ferland is unfazed. As he likes to say, "I'm one happy Head Pineapple."

Pierre's Points for Being Successful in Another Country

✓ Do your homework, learn about the market, the labour force, work permits, and taxes.

✓ Choose a business you have experience and passion in because you can't rely on someone else to run it for you.

✓ Check your supply sources and adapt to what you can acquire in your geographic region.

✓ Have self-discipline and stay away from tourist temptations like gambling and drugs.

✓ Balance your family life with work. I give two hundred percent every time I'm here, but I have two kids and I just want to be a perfect dad.

Invest in Yourself

Lisa Larter
Founder and CEO of The Lisa Larter Group

Lisa Larter calls herself the Accidental Expert.

"One day the F-word showed up on my BlackBerry and I thought 'Oh God, now I'm going to have to learn Facebook.' I thought it was for kids and cheating spouses," Lisa says, laughing.

Larter has built a business empire based on connecting through social media. The petite, bubbly blonde with a love for anything pink commands attention, but the smart, savvy businesswoman's hazel eyes turn the color of steel when she talks about succeeding in the outside world.

Born in Oromocto, New Brunswick, Lisa's parents separated when she was in grade four. Moving with her mom to Ontario, they settled in Haliburton, a picturesque summer community popular with cottagers and boaters. Money was tight so Lisa decided to get a part-time job.

"I was hired and fired within twenty-four hours," she says honestly. "I was twelve years old and while I was able to get a job at the Banks General Store, they fired me because I wasn't old enough to work. I had to be thirteen to get a social insurance number."

The experience didn't faze Larter. Handy with a crochet needle, she decided to go into business for herself.

"I made hearts, snowmen, Easter bunnies, and Santa Clauses into pins. I crocheted baby blankets and afghans. I collected my old books, toys, and things I didn't want anymore and took them to the flea market. My mom came too, and didn't sell anything, but I walked away with a lot of cash," she says, smiling.

From the experience at the flea market, Larter learned a valuable life lesson. She knew she could sell.

"You have to be able to communicate with people. I also learned if you don't have confidence in what you're selling, how can you expect others to have confidence in what you do?"

At age eighteen, she moved to Ottawa to live with her dad, however, there were many challenges and Lisa dropped out of high school.

"My father was very upset," she recalls, "and told me I didn't have what it takes to go to university, so I found a job in retail selling women's clothing."

Over the next few years, Larter powered up the ladder, moving from associate to store manager. Switching to wireless phones, she helped open thirty-one stores in six months and within two years was promoted to Regional Manager. With a team doing one hundred million dollars in sales, Lisa was successful, making good money, and thinking about taking the next step.

"I always knew I wanted my own business. I just didn't know what it was."

Remembering her flea market days, Lisa began a sideline, selling gift baskets filled with organic chocolates and teas.

"I was bringing in thirty thousand dollars a year with a part-time venture. That told me I could make money in a business on my own. In the corporate world there was the glass ceiling, plus I was tired of traveling, so I thought, 'why not open up a TELUS store?'"

Surrounded by wireless phones, Larter began to explore the latest social media craze. When Facebook showed up on her BlackBerry she had no idea her career was about to take a dramatic new turn.

"There I was, selling phones with apps and the latest, greatest features that I didn't understand. I went home that night and signed up for Facebook," Lisa recalls. "I realized I could connect and market to people more effectively than the traditional ways I was used to."

Shortly after mastering social media, Larter went to a women's networking luncheon and was shocked when someone offered to pay her if Lisa taught her how Facebook and Twitter worked.

"I thought, 'Hmmm, I'm on to something.' I offered a beginner's course and ten people signed up."

Her new social media venture began to take off, and Larter became so busy she hired a manager to look after the phone store.

"In the corporate world, you don't know how much value you have to others because you are in it. It wasn't until I was a part of the small business community that I knew what my contribution would be."

The workshops became half and full day programs, morphing into private consulting work.

"I landed a retail shopping centre client and that's when I saw how I could add value to an organization on a different level. I began by teaching people which buttons to press, and now I am linking social media with sales and marketing."

Larter also began writing a blog and newsletter. Her workshops and consulting business grew and it wasn't long before she recognized the need for help. Hiring an assistant was a huge step and Lisa says it was a key factor in getting her newest venture off the ground.

"It was a leap of faith to invest in myself. I realized early you can't do it alone. People may think they have to do everything but you eventually get further away from what you do best. I hate cleaning my house, so I hire someone to do it. It's the same thing in business. If you hire, you can focus on your strengths and generate revenue for your company."

Larter recently sold the phone store to concentrate on combining her unique skills of retail, wireless, and social media, and now leads a focused team of ten employees.

"Social media is an opportunity to be more strategic about business, but I find we're using it like TV and not using it to engage. We're talking at people instead of with them, broadcasting our message like TV did in the '70's, and expecting to get the same results."

Larter has learned many critical lessons from social media including how it can be applied when running a company. She doesn't want to be a 1980's consultant unable to connect with people in the twenty-first century.

"A woman came up to me and said, 'I've been watching you for the last two years and I'm jealous because I'm not as far along in my business.'

"The difference? I'm focused on relationships and how to help people. She's focusing on what's in it for her and not for other people. I have built amazing relationships over the past four years and it's helped to elevate my online presence, reputation, and credibility."

Larter follows key principles when approaching the corporate world.

"You need courage, the right skills, and abilities to do what you need to do. This is where a lot of people fall down. They'll invest in bricks and mortar but are afraid to invest in themselves. You also need self-confidence, and the more competent you become, the more confident you will be. You must invest in learning. You must create strong habits in your personal life and your business. Do the things that matter and do them every day so your business will grow. Become fanatical about understanding your numbers, because if you can't measure results then it doesn't matter."

Larter also believes a good coach and mentor can help bring your company to the next level.

"I believe we're too close to our businesses and we need other people to target things we don't see. If you hire an expert, make sure you are ready and willing to be coached. Listen to the feedback, and then take action. Big growth doesn't come from focusing on little things."

Larter also advises ignoring the inner chatter in our heads because it can strip away confidence.

"We all second guess ourselves, have doubts and insecurities. You have a choice. You can listen to the chatter and be paralyzed, or you can acknowledge it and take action. You have to do the work to get where you want to go."

Goal setting is also important to Larter. "I don't have a vision board, however, every year I set goals so bold they scare me. Then I try to make them happen. Not reaching them is not an option," she says with conviction. "I believe if you really want something you can make it happen. I didn't get from that little apartment in Oromocto to where I am now by giving up easily."

Larter's consulting company has become so profitable she owns three homes and has a shared partnership in a commercial building. Lisa has the financial freedom many of us can only dream about.

"There has never been a better time to be in business because we've never been able to access people like we can today. Act in spite of your fear. When you push through, there's magic on the other side."

Lisa Larter's C.A.S.H. Model

COURAGE - Take a risk and act on it or your idea will always remain a dream.

APTITUDE - Invest in yourself because you need the right skills and tools to be successful.

SELF-CONFIDENCE – It comes from courage and gaining the aptitude you need to succeed.

HABITS - You need to apply strong habits for your business to grow. Systems and routines for getting things done make a tremendous difference in the results you accomplish.

Give Back_____

Royson Ng
President, Samtack Inc.

"Canada is a goldmine of opportunity," says Royson Ng, from his large corner office at Samtack Inc. Now the award winning entrepreneur and businessman is inspiring other new immigrants to become entrepreneurs and is leading by example.

Ng grew up in Malaysia where his dad ran a watch shop, and Royson would help out by running errands and changing watch straps. His mom also made sure he knew the value of work and money by encouraging him to find cardboard and take it to the recycling centre to be exchanged for cash. In his late teens, Royson reached a critical moment in his life; he wanted to go to England to finish his education.

"My dad wanted his kids to take over the business," Royson tells me. "I was the black sheep of the family and said, 'Dad, I have to go.' My mom and sister helped me financially but my dad wouldn't. I took my savings and left."

Royson put himself through the London School of Accounting and then completed a business administration degree course. While working at an accounting firm, he pursued his master's degree. After marrying and having a child, Royson and his wife were looking to put down permanent roots in England, but the approval process for residency was difficult. Ng applied to live in Canada and was approved immediately as a skilled worker. Still, it took four years before the paperwork was completed and Royson moved his family to Toronto.

They arrived in the middle of winter and, with his wife expecting their second child, he had to find work quickly. Royson reflects back to the early days, becoming thoughtful. "My biggest setback was not having any Canadian experience. They told me, 'You have a degree. So what?' As a result, they didn't judge me for who I am, they judged me by paper."

Ng pumped gas, repaired clocks and found a job working at Future Shop. He was much older than the average employee and lacked computer experience. Royson knew how to sell, but he didn't know how computers worked, so if a customer came in with a technical problem, Ng was stuck. He talked to the other employees and struck a deal. When a customer came in with a problem, his coworkers would fix it for Royson, while he went into selling mode for them. Any commission earned went to the employee who helped him. Within three months, he learned the technical side of the computer business and had caught the attention of head office. Royson had made such an impression that he was fast tracked through to management.

"When I was regional marketing manager, I found a company that could supply computers to Future Shop. I was instrumental in bringing Samtack to them and the owner wanted me to run his company in Canada. The offer was very good and I jumped on board."

After Royson's arrival in the corner office, Samtack's revenue soared from 20 million a year to over 400 million worldwide.

"Today, Samtack has changed significantly. It was a computer company but five years ago we changed, and we now have everything from food, health items, consumer electronics, toys, and furniture. We are a distributor and a logistic fulfillment house. You can go to a client's website and buy from them, but the order actually comes to Samtack without you knowing it."

The biggest names in the retail world like Walmart, Best Buy, Future Shop, Sears, and Home Depot rely on Samtack's services and Royson's expertise.

"Samtack also does reverse logistics. Things that don't sell, I take back for refurbishing. I then sell them back to the end user at 50% of the original price and I'm still able to offer them warranty."

While he enjoys the corner office at Samtack Inc., and the title of President, Royson still considers himself an entrepreneur. He is a partner and owner of the company and mentors others to pursue their goals in business.

"I have become an entrepreneur because of what I have learned. A good way to become successful is to work for someone, understand their culture, and learn their business before you embark on starting your own company."

Royson particularly wants to help immigrants and people new to the country. Today, 97% of all Samtack employees are new Canadians, and he's brutally honest with them when they arrive looking for work.

"I tell them, 'You think you were very good where you came from? Well, forget it, burn the bridge, and move on.'"

The advice may seem harsh, however, Royson believes it's better to get a dose of reality than to end up broke with no job prospects and having to leave Canada. Ng draws on his own personal journey and doles out honesty and tough love to new immigrants, but he also gives them hope.

"There is a lot of gold in Canada. When someone gives you an opportunity you have to grab it, even if the pay is low. Then keep trying and think that nothing can stop you. A lot of people who immigrate here go back home within a few years. The key is to tell someone what your dream is, and be sure you tell the right people. Talk to a bank manager, a consultant, or a mentor. Take the first step and put it into action.

"People are more entrepreneurial than they ever were. I take a lot of calls and talk to many people. It's all about networking," Royson says. "You also have to be patient and believe it will work. There are ups and downs, and you'll need persistence and a positive attitude to make it in business."

Ng also believes a key to success is being reachable at all hours. Regardless of where he may be traveling, customer calls are always answered because Royson believes they have the right to get in touch with him when problems arise.

"I'm reachable 365 hours, 24 hours a day. I may be in the U.K., but I never say, 'I'm away.' If your customer wants to communicate, you need to be there to take their calls even if they need to complain. You must learn how to be tactful, but I am always available to my customers."

No matter how busy he is, Royson also values the days he spends with his wife and children. They enjoy family time together and take vacations, however, he is also teaching them the basic principles of business.

"I had my sons deliver newspapers because we want them to understand the value of money and how hard it is to earn it. It gave us good bonding."

Royson still has big plans for himself and Samtack Inc.

"I don't know if I will ever retire. At this stage, I'm looking at a lot of new companies because I don't believe all businesses are sustainable if they don't evolve. Every five years you must have a new business."

Ng loves every aspect of Samtack, but takes particular pride in helping others reach their entrepreneurial goals.

"Giving money is one thing, but I believe that you should also give a part of yourself. I get a lot of satisfaction from that."

Royson Ng's Five "F" Culture of Success

✓ Fast to market, deliver, and turn it around fast.

✓ Focus on what you do for your employees, the market, your customers, and profitability.

✓ Flexible in everything you do because if you're not, you won't evolve and will become stagnant.

✓ Friendly with customers, as well as employees, and have an open door policy so people enjoy working with you.

✓ Fun - make your company a fun place to work by hosting BBQ days, parties, and taking employees on adventures.

Triumph Over Adversity

Jeff Collins
CEO and President
K-9 Orthotics and Prosthetics Inc.

There was nothing more the paramedics could do for the accident victim bleeding on the stretcher. The man's injuries were horrific and he had no vital signs. As the medic sadly punched in the letters D.O.A., Dead On Arrival, into the computer, Jeff Collins' eyes flashed open and he sat up. "I'm okay," he told the stunned medical crew, then fell back onto the stretcher and passed out.

Jeff is very honest when he talks about the motorcycle crash that dramatically changed his life. As Collins reflects back on the accident, you marvel at how a man's darkest hour can turn into a time of triumph and reinvention.

"I was twenty years old and facing seven months in a rehab facility," Collins tells me from his home near Halifax. His right leg was badly damaged and after five months of surgeries they had to amputate. The other leg was shattered and had to be rebuilt using steel plates and wire. One of Jeff's arms was also mangled and required extensive surgery and physiotherapy. As he fought through the pain and rehabilitation to heal his broken body, Collins questioned the journey that had been put in front of him. He had no idea his healing process would lead him to create groundbreaking technology that would one day be used around the world. All of the exciting travel, speeches, and conferences were were down the road. For now, he just had to get his body put back together again.

"I needed a custom prosthesis made for my amputated leg," Jeff says, as he recalls the early days of his recovery. "It was challenging because I had a lot of clinical issues, and had to go through many surgeries. No one was able to make me feel comfortable and the pain was unbearable."

After months of frustration, Collins decided to learn how to make the prosthetic leg himself. He enrolled at a college in Toronto, packed up, and left his home in Nova Scotia. Jeff enjoyed his school and the company of his new classmates, however, after another surgery on his amputated leg, he ended up with a terrible infection. His new friends banded together to look after him.

"I lived on their couch for a week. A nurse in the building took care of me because I had a fever due to the infection. My stubbornness pushed me through it, but I still hit rock bottom, the lowest you can go. I reached the point where I told myself, 'Something has gotta give or something's gotta change.' I'm a firm believer you're the creator of your own destiny and you have to stay focused."

Collins was ready to turn his life around.

After graduation, Jeff became a Pediatric Prosthetic Specialist helping children adapt to their new mobility. The work was rewarding, but he missed his family and friends in Nova Scotia. Jeff gave up his job and moved back home. Collins was unemployed and still didn't have a prosthetic leg, but there was a plan in place. He was going to start his own company.

"I had a meeting with the rehab specialists, nurses, and doctors. I was in a room with all these professionals. One of the doctors told me I had unrealistic ambitions and I should rethink them. He said I should take it easy and not be as active as I am."

Collins was angry the doctors had put limitations on his progress.

"I was really bugged by the doctor's comments. I thought he should inspire me and other patients."

Deciding not to listen to the doctor's advice, Collins enrolled in Dalhousie University's Continuing Education program and wrote a business plan for starting a private orthotic company. Money was tight; however, life was once again looking better for Collins until his dog Stash, a black lab mix he had rescued off the streets of Toronto, began limping. The diagnosis was a torn

ACL and she needed surgery to repair it.

"Here I am in limbo, on unemployment insurance, and waiting for my prosthetic leg to be made. I couldn't afford surgery on Stash's knee. My dog was suffering and I had to find a way to help her."

As he looked down into Stash's trusting eyes, the solution to his current dilemma hit him. Using the human techniques he had learned, Collins went to work, and within a few days Stash was walking around pain free sporting a new knee brace.

There were other dogs needing Collins' help and soon he had a stable of new, four-legged patients. K-9 Orthotics and Prosthetics was in business. He made twenty devices the first year and the new company took off. People were buzzing about his work and revolutionary designs. Invitations from animal health conferences around the world began to pour in. Collins traveled to Sweden, Switzerland, the Netherlands, Germany, Chile, and throughout the U.S. giving lectures on his revolutionary designs and showing veterinarians how to use animal prosthetics.

"People were coming to me for advice. I had a thriving, prosperous company in a new market. I was also working with veterinarians to have my knowledge incorporated into their textbooks."

The following years were filled with expansion, growth, and addition of new staff members to keep up with the incoming orders. Then in 2010, the train came off the tracks. A series of issues developed, threatening to derail everything Collins had built.

"I came close to going out of business," Jeff says honestly. "I had staffing issues when I lost several technical employees and I had to hire and train new personnel."

He also developed problems with two senior technicians and the new employees weren't getting the guidance they needed. To complicate matters, the senior staffers were close, personal friends. Collins realized he had to make a tough decision.

"I shook the ship and changed the crew. It put us in a bad position. We were at our highest peak of production and sales when it all happened. It was a risky gamble and I ended up putting in long hours."

Collins' travel schedule was as demanding as ever. Pushing himself to the limit, he was trying to do it all when another health crisis struck.

"I was at a conference in Las Vegas and accidentally pushed myself off a chair, breaking three vertebrae and a rib. I ended up back home in Nova Scotia for four weeks while I healed."

Still not fully recovered, Collins traveled to a veterinarian conference in Chicago, and damaged his amputated leg due to overuse. Shortly after, he flew to Florida to speak at another conference and take part in a TV show. With ongoing staffing issues back home, Collins realized the perfect storm was gathering and he was headed for a tsunami of trouble.

"There was a direct impact on sales and cash flow because I was incapacitated for a few months. I knew I had to get a little breathing room with the lenders to rebuild my company."

Collins was direct and frank when he met with the bankers and told them about his situation.

"I had been working hard at the business for seven years and sales had grown every year. I asked them to look at my history, and work with me. Or, I told them, they could take legal action against me which would take a long time and they'd end up with nothing." Jeff pauses for a moment, and then says confidently, "They gave me six months."

Collins pulled the company back together and says K-9 Orthotics and Prosthetics is once again thriving.

"We've sprung back very well," Collins says energetically. "The business is flourishing and I'm in discussions with a company to take over the manufacturing of some of my products because, right now, I have more sales than I can produce. I already have a company in Ottawa making our wheelchairs."

Collins is also working with his international clients to bring them together globally to advance the training and technology related to canine animals at a prosthetic and rehab level. He's also sourcing out pre-designed product for production, and focusing on custom training.

Jeff's personal life is also thriving. He met a veterinarian from Chile in North Carolina several years ago. "She was finalizing her certification in canine rehab and I met her at a private clinic. Within eight months she was living with me in Nova Scotia, and a year and a half ago we had our first baby girl," Jeff says, his voice filling with pride.

It's been quite the journey and Collins is willing to share what he's learned.

"You are in charge of your own destiny," Collins says thoughtfully and with conviction. "When you're going through life and find yourself in a negative state, remind yourself this is a passing phase of emotions and you'll get into a more positive frame of mind. We're never going to be filled with one hundred percent joy all the time, so don't let negativity get you down. It'll pass."

Collins pauses and reflects for a moment about life and business. "If it was easy, everyone would do it. Expect challenges and hardship. The harder it gets, the more inspiring it will be. Have a strong work ethic, and expect nothing to go as planned. I'm always changing my business plan."

Paperwork aside, his patients bring him the most satisfaction. A shepherd mix, named Kayla, has a new prosthetic leg after her paw was caught in a hunter's trap. A championship dog in Latvia has a custom knee brace, and canine war vets have been given new hope after injuring their legs and paws on the battlefield. Collins has also used his technology to help other animals including cats, rabbits, llamas, and even a moose.

Today, Jeff Collins celebrates the accident and the day that changed his life because it marked a turning point for him and the groundbreaking technology he pioneered. His patients bring him joy and fulfillment on the job. "They look up at me with eyes of gratitude and wagging tails," Jeff says with a smile. "I'm so happy I can help these animals."

Collins' Thoughts on Success

✓ Be ready to work very hard and put in long hours.

✓ Avoid using family and friends as investors or employees.

✓ Listen, engage, and empower your workers as much as possible. Without them you will not succeed.

✓ Harness and utilize the chaos and stresses of being an entrepreneur. You will make mistakes but it is imperative to remember the lessons learned.

✓ Take nothing for granted and always be dynamic.

Reinvent Yourself

Charmaine Hammond
Speaker, Corporate Trainer,
and Best Selling Author

Chris Alcock opened the door to his Edmonton home and thought he was walking into a crime scene. Water was everywhere, plants had been knocked over, and black, gooey mud covered the rug. Furniture had been moved to different rooms, knives were scattered over the blood spattered floor, and all their clothing had been ripped out of closets and thrown into a pile. In the bathroom, every tap had been turned on and the porcelain toilet lid was on the ground smashed into jagged pieces. As Chris surveyed all the damage, he wondered who or what had caused so much destruction. Then he looked down. Staring at him with baleful eyes filled with anxiety and sadness was his ninety pound rescue dog, Toby.

Chris picked up the phone and called his wife, Charmaine.

"You're never going to believe what YOUR dog did today," he said tiredly into the receiver.

The Alcock-Hammond home was destroyed and they had no idea the event would be the beginning of a wonderful adventure filled with business opportunities, awards, and even a call from Hollywood. All the good stuff was yet to come. All Charmaine saw when she walked through the front door was one big mess.

The couple looked at each other. What had happened to the loveable, happy Chesapeake Bay Retriever they had taken in from the animal rescue organization?

"Toby was five when we adopted him and we learned he had been with an older couple," Charmaine tells me, recalling the beginning of her odyssey. "Unfortunately, the man had a heart attack and died. His wife couldn't care for the dog anymore so she had to give him away. It had a damaging effect on Toby and he ended up with anxiety and separation disorder."

Desperate for answers, Hammond went to see an animal behaviourist. Once Charmaine was done explaining, the expert thought for a moment and then said, "Toby is uncertain with his role in your family. Your dog needs a job."

Helping the mentally wounded reinvent themselves was nothing new for Charmaine. A career in the prison system as a corrections officer, a job in a young offenders' facility, and work at a women's shelter had given Hammond many useful skills. Could they be used on a dog? Looking into his troubled, amber eyes, Charmaine was determined to help the dog find peace in his life. Little did she know Toby's journey would impact thousands of lives and change her world dramatically.

Hammond was introduced to the Chimo Project, a respected animal assisted therapy program in Edmonton. Sporting a bright red bandana and a special dog vest, they began visiting hospitals. Toby loved wearing his uniform and interacting with the patients. Then his enthusiasm spilled over and his sharp bark echoed down the corridors causing people to get upset. It looked as if all the doors were closing for Toby when a friend suggested they apply to work at the psychiatric hospital. Toby was an immediate hit at the facility as he began spreading love and companionship to people with mental illnesses, and his loud bark actually helped rouse several patients out of the haze of their crippling disease. Soon they were lining up to take the lovable, big dog out for a walk or play fetch with him. Toby had found his purpose in life; he had a job.

"A bunch of serendipitous things happened," Charmaine says excitedly. "I was speaking in San Diego and met a publisher. She asked me to write a chapter on mother/daughter conflict for a book she was working on but I didn't do a good job. Here was a successful woman who had published thirty-six books, some of which had been made into movies and I blew it. I was so angry at myself. Over dinner she asked me about *my* life. I started telling her how our dog was driving us crazy but he was also becoming a teacher of rich lessons in life and business. She said, 'There's the book. Now get writing.'"

Hammond returned to Edmonton and stared at the empty pad of paper. She didn't know how to write a book and there was no time to learn.

"I felt the same way as I did when walking through the jail the first time," Charmaine said, recalling her early days as a corrections officer. "I was scared, excited, and I had no concept of what to do. Chris suggested I just start writing, but I ended up with one big run-on story. We hired several editors to help me frame the outline and I completed it in six months. I was such a perfectionist, but I knew I had to let it go. It was one of the lessons Toby was teaching me. I had to send it in and move forward."

The day *On Toby's Terms* arrived was a momentous occasion for the Hammond family. Toby did his happy dance around the big box as if he knew the book was all about him.

"I'll never forget the first time we did a book signing," Charmaine says breaking into a huge smile. "I walked into our local Chapters store and there was a lineup of people. Toby was so excited. We had a spring-loaded *pawtograph* machine so he could sign the books. He looked up at me and at that moment I realized, this is my life. This is totally what I'm meant to do right now."

Toby became a celebrity, appearing on TV and in newspapers. Hollywood also was calling. Charmaine signed a contract with a production company based in Los Angeles to turn Toby's story into a movie.

"Along with the book signings, Toby and I did charity events, speaking tours, and went into schools. There was more reinvention as the whole Toby part of our world started to take over. My speaking opportunities increased and I was sharing stories about our dog in my presentations. His stories were connecting people."

For five years, Toby faithfully looked after Charmaine and Chris, ministered to his patients and visited ten thousand school children to promote literacy and kindness. *On Toby's Terms* became a best seller, and in 2010 he won the Chimo Reese Award for his outstanding volunteer work.

"When it came to people," Charmaine says, "Toby connected through the heart."

The lovable dog was ten and a half years old when he passed away in November of 2011, leaving behind a legacy of compassion, learning, and sharing. Toby also left a trail of broken hearts of those who loved him the most.

"He was so gentle, kind, and loving," Charmaine says in a quiet voice filled with pride. "When I watched him start his day with his crazy, happy dance, it taught me how you show up in life and business is very important. For Toby, every moment was filled with joy and it was the best day in the world. I started becoming more present in my life and stopped trying to orchestrate the future. For once, I let life and work happen."

She has written three children's books featuring the personable dog, dealing with literacy and bullying. The movie is in the works, and in 2012 they launched Toby's Global Mission – A Million Acts of Kindness.

"He lived a big life and impacted hearts around the world," Charmaine says. "His mission is so important and we must continue it. We want to show schools, workplaces, and communities the importance of kindness and how it can change lives."

Hammond is living proof of how anyone, even a dog, can reinvent themselves in life and business.

"There is always a bit of fear about transformation," she says thoughtfully. "If life tests you, then you know you are going in the right direction. Every time I reinvented myself I thought, 'What if doesn't work? Or if it does, what will I do if it takes off?' It's okay. A little bit of fear keeps you connected with what is going on in your life.

"It's critical for leaders to be able to completely transform or reinvent their business. If I had hung on to the status quo in my life and career and resisted change then there are a gazillion things I wouldn't have done. I was always waiting for the perfect opportunity, however, I found out it doesn't exist. The timing is now and you have to step into it."

Jack Canfield, a motivational speaker and author best known for co-creating the Chicken Soup for the Soul book series, gave Hammond advice she took to heart.

"Connect with what your passion is. If it doesn't excite you it may not be a project you should say yes to. Have big shoulders and say no. Jack Canfield said, 'If your hands are busy hanging onto the good then there's no room for the amazing.'

"Be open to the fact your dreams and goals will change throughout life," Charmaine suggests. "As we become seasoned business owners there are times when our passion becomes bigger. It's about being open to that."

Life is a continual process of change, renewal, and metamorphosis. However, the key lesson we can learn from Charmaine and Toby is inspiration can come in many different forms. Even from our four legged friends.

"He came into my life to be a teacher and there are still lessons we reflect on through Toby. People need to be open to the beautiful gifts animals can bring."

Reinvention and transformation, a fitting tribute to a determined dog who left an indelible paw print on everyone's heart.

Lessons Charmaine Learned from Toby

✓ Perseverance and Commitment. Toby never gave up.

✓ Stop being a perfectionist. Life opens up when we don't expect everything to be perfect.

✓ The power of kindness. I would watch Toby connect with people, and it was such a deep, beautiful sharing of kindness.

✓ Unconditional acceptance. Toby never judged, he accepted people for who they were and where they were at that moment.

✓ Hope. In the most difficult of days, it will carry you through.

Persevere

Ingrid Laederach Steven
Owner of Swiss-Master Chocolatier

The beautiful little chocolate shop is tucked into a strip mall in one of Toronto's most exclusive neighbourhoods. On the front door is a sign with the saying, "I Believe … that you can keep going long after you think you can't." The author of the quote is unknown, but it is the mantra of the owner, a woman as beautiful as the tasty chocolates she has sold for the last twenty-seven years.

When you first meet Ingrid Laederach Steven, you have no idea how many traumatic turning points have shaped her life. All you see is a charming woman radiating inner peace and dispensing wonderful bits of advice along with her decadent chocolates. Ingrid's message is simple: you must persevere in business and life no matter what challenges you face, and you must never lose your faith in people.

"I was born in Lucerne, Switzerland, and lived in the Alps," Ingrid tells me from across the table in a busy Toronto restaurant. We have found a quiet corner away from the lunchtime bustle, and as she tells me her story I'm struck at how gentle and soft spoken she is. Ingrid is a picture of European elegance with sandy blonde hair and warm brown eyes. "My parents were in the tourism business and I didn't see them as much as I wanted to. My biggest dream as a child was to have children and a nice home where we gathered for family celebrations and dinners.

"I was sent to school at a convent and although the nuns were good to me I used to get into a lot of trouble. I was put on toilet cleaning duty a lot," she recalls, smiling at the memory.

Being away from her mother and father at such a young age was difficult, however, the precocious child learned many valuable skills while at the convent and developed a love for music. Back home one summer helping her parents, she started singing to herself not realizing there were other people in the room.

"The conductor of the Denver Symphony Orchestra heard me. She sought out my parents and said, 'This girl has a gift. I want to take her back to the U.S. so she can study.'"

Ingrid was only eleven years old, and it was a tremendous opportunity. The decision was made, her clothes were packed, and she went to live with the conductor in Denver. She didn't speak English and the transition was hard for the young girl, but her talent and flair for music seemed to smooth the way.

"I traveled throughout the United States performing and I loved it. I felt a real euphoria when I heard the audiences clap. I wanted people to be proud of me. The first time I performed on TV I thought I was going to pass out, but I made it. We even traveled to California."

Ingrid stops for a moment and collects herself before continuing.

"She was trying to make something out of me and I was more than willing, yet there was a resistance building in me. I didn't want to be molded and I just wanted to go back home. I was only twelve years old and felt trapped. It was real low point in my life and I felt I had no real support or love so I decided to end it all. I went to the conductor's medicine cabinet and swallowed all the pills I could find."

Ingrid was in a coma for two weeks. Lying paralyzed in a hospital bed, she heard the doctors talking urgently in the room. "We're not sure how much longer she's going to live and we have to get her parents here now!" Something snapped in Ingrid at that moment and she began to will her body back to life.

"I said to myself, 'I have to get out of this!'" Ingrid gradually woke from the coma, but the damage to her brain and body was severe. For the next two months she had to re-learn how to do everything including how to walk, talk, feed, and dress herself. The gifted girl who had dazzled television audiences across the United States with her impressive singing voice was silenced. With damaged vocal chords, Ingrid never sang again.

Looking for a new start, she moved to Toronto with her parents. This time the transition was smoother for the teen. She went to school and developed lasting friendships. At the age of seventeen, she went to a dance at the local YMCA with a girlfriend and met a man named Tom Steven.

"He was handsome, tall, and had kind eyes. We dated and continued to see each other. I remember we were driving one day and Tom saw a handicapped person struggling to get across the street. He stopped the car, and jumped out to help get the person to safety. I thought to myself, 'this is the man for me.' We were married when I was twenty."

It appeared Ingrid had finally found the stability and life she had been yearning for. Yet, her journey was about take another strange and dangerous turn. Flying back from a trip to Arizona, Ingrid became ill on the plane. A well-meaning flight attendant gave her oxygen, but the effects of the altitude and extra oxygen put her into cardiac arrest. There was a doctor on board the plane, and while the pilots worked on making an emergency landing, Ingrid fought to stay alive. She remembers looking at her distraught husband and thinking, "He'll be okay, he's young. He can marry again." Once the plane was on the ground they raced to the hospital.

"My body became heavy and I went into a tunnel toward a beautiful light. There was music playing and it was amazing. I looked back on them working on my body and I felt no pain. I went further into the tunnel, then realized I had to go back. I knew I had no choice. It was a horrible feeling and I felt like I was being sucked through a vacuum cleaner. It was at that moment I heard the doctor yell, 'She's back – we've got her!'"

Twice in her young life Ingrid had cheated death. She tried to move forward and create the family they had yearned for, but the medical issues continued.

"Tom and I wanted to have children but I went through seven miscarriages, and it broke my spirit and my heart. Some of the babies lived. I started making all kinds of bargains with God. I said, 'If you let this baby live, I will do anything.' It wasn't meant to be and when I had to bury them, it was heartbreaking."

Her seventh child lived three days before she had to say goodbye. Through the darkness and days of dashed hope and profound sadness, Ingrid refused to give in to the negativity surrounding her life.

"I kept persevering," Ingrid says, "I kept telling myself, 'It's going to happen – it's going to happen.'"

Ingrid's prayers were answered. Shortly after she wrote the poem she became pregnant again, and this time her beautiful baby daughter was born healthy. Three years later, she was five months pregnant with her second child, when the doctors walked into her hospital room with devastating news.

"The doctors told me that due to my history and the medication they had given me, there was a strong chance my child might be born with severe problems. They told me to consider an abortion. For me it was not an option. I told them absolutely not."

After months of bed rest in hospital, Ingrid and Tom's second daughter was born. She was tiny, but strong, and had no health issues. Her faith and prayers had been answered. The Laederach Steven family was complete.

Ingrid remembered back to the early days in Switzerland when she longed for a family to love and call her own. She had beaten the odds and had come back from death's door twice. Through it all she remained positive, and decided it was time for the next challenge. Laederach Steven was going to open a business.

Drawing inspiration from her family heritage, Ingrid began importing cookies from Switzerland.

"My father always encouraged me to look into the family chocolate business. I was at a food show in New York when I ran into my Great Uncle. We sat down to talk about Laederach Chocolates. I decided to import the 'best of the best' and it was the beginning of Swiss-Master Chocolatier."

Ingrid opened a small shop near one of Canada's wealthiest neighbourhoods. The Bridle Path is filled with multi-million dollar homes set on huge parcels of land behind imposing black iron gates and tall hedges. Celebrities, giants of business, and members of Canada's wealthiest families call the area home. Swiss-Master Chocolatier fit right in to the affluent neighbourhood, offering decadent truffles filled with the best ingredients money could buy. The showcases were filled with decadent morsels of chocolate perfection and every Christmas, Easter, and Valentine's Day, the shop exploded in a riot of color, decoration, and whimsy.

"I had to be in an area where people appreciated the quality. The first years were tough, however. People didn't understand the product and why it was so expensive so I had to show them why.

"We had a recession in 1982 and it took five years for the shop to turn a profit. I thought if I gave up immediately then I wasn't gaining anything so I persisted and kept going."

Ingrid nurtured her business and built a loyal clientele. It wasn't uncommon to see Hollywood celebrities in the shop along with thousands of people who have discovered the mouth-watering joy chocolate brings. Presidents, royalty, a pope, and astronauts have all nibbled Swiss-Master Chocolatier's amazing truffles and treats.

"One day a short man with a bodyguard came into the shop. He was very nice and asked me questions about the chocolates, then picked out what he wanted. After his bodyguard paid, they left. I noticed there were a lot of people out front of the shop and finally one of the girls ran in, saying, 'Do you know who was in your store?' I had no clue. Then she yelled, 'That was Prince!' Other people had to tell me he was a famous performer and movie star."

It doesn't matter if you're rock royalty or someone working down the street, everyone is treated with the same warmth and compassion at Swiss-Master Chocolatier.

"We've now been through three recessions. Our demographics have changed so we had to bring in new product. During one recession I designed a happy face truffle to make people feel better. I try to think like a customer rather than an owner because then I can understand exactly what someone wants. We deliver top service, quality, and kindness."

Through all of life's setbacks and severe health challenges, Ingrid's philosophy remains as sunny and sweet as her chocolate.

"I tell people not to give up. Life does get better. You can have dreams, however, don't make them too far out of reach so you can't attain them. You have to be realistic, but good things do happen.

"Every day I realize I'm lucky." Ingrid says with pride. "So lucky."

As we look at Ingrid's life we realize we're the lucky ones. She's shown us not all turning points in life are happy ones, however, with a little dose of optimism, hope – and a few chocolates – we can all persevere and "Believe."

Ingrid's Sweet Success Formula

✓ Be honest.

✓ Be sincere.

✓ Think like a customer.

✓ Be consistent and persevere.

✓ Make your place a happy one.

Be Fearless

Wally Mah
President and Co-Owner
North Ridge Development

"You are absolutely crazy to even consider going into real estate development right now." Wally Mah stared at his supervisor at the Canada Revenue Agency in Saskatoon and looked around at the office he had toiled in for years. Needing more guidance he called his father, but his reaction to Wally's plan wasn't much better.

"The only thing they obviously didn't teach you at school was how to count," his dad told him sternly. "Interest rates are at twenty-two percent!"

It was 1982, and with the country in the grips of a recession and interest rates skyrocketing, Mah knew it wasn't the right time to quit his comfortable job as an auditor with the government. However, he didn't want to be stuck in a job he didn't enjoy.

"I worked with a lot of auditors and watched them retire. They weren't satisfied at the end of their career with what they had done. It was a life-changing moment when I thought, 'This could be me.' I wanted to do something else."

Wally considered his options and decided to pull the plug on his job at the CRA. The only one who believed in his plan was his wife.

"I met Colleen at university when I borrowed her library card and didn't return it," Mah says, laughing. "Now we were married, with a newborn son, yet she knew I wasn't happy. She looked at me and said, 'If this is what you want to do, I'll support you.'"

To start his company, Wally needed financial backing and he found it at the CRA office. Jules Calyniuk was also interested in getting into real estate but he didn't want to quit his day job. Wally and Jules took out a loan on their used cars, found a plot of land, and started to build a duplex. Mah wasn't afraid of hard work or getting his hands dirty. He remembered back to his early days in Prince Albert, Saskatchewan, when he worked long hours with his four siblings in the family-owned restaurant. He knew how to paint and swing a hammer.

"We used subcontractors but did a lot of the work ourselves," Wally recalls. "We put in the insulation, did the painting, laid the blocks, built a fence and the decks. We couldn't find a plumber because they were so busy with the big builders. Finally, a friend who lived ninety miles away pulled in a favour, convincing a plumber to work for us."

With their first duplex completed and rented, Mah and Calyniuk continued to expand. In the next few years, they built thirty rental units, keeping eighteen and selling the rest. By the mid-eighties the economy had turned around and North Ridge Development was doing well. As the leading force in the company, Wally was a visionary and wasn't afraid of taking a risk.

"In 1989, we decided to build condos and townhouses. It had never been done in Saskatoon. We have so much land and people didn't accept this form of housing. I thought the townhouses were affordable and would cater to first-time home buyers. We even decided to build a daycare for the complex. It turned out I was dead wrong. Ninety percent of the people buying the units were seniors who were downsizing. I had a lightbulb moment. What you presume to be reality may not be what's needed at all."

For the next ten years Mah kept building townhouses. His friends thought he was out of his mind and many of his peers thought he'd go broke.

"Every time we put a project together, it sold. We were building city blocks full of townhouses and custom homes."

Mah's leadership and vision put him on the map and gave him financial security. He was a man who had it all; a supportive wife, two beautiful sons, and a thriving company. Then his whole world fell apart.

"I went into a partnership with my son's godfather in the early1990's. We built a project in Edmonton and, trusting this man, I gave him single signing authority. He cleaned out the bank account and took the mortgage to the maximum, threatening, 'You can sue me if you want but I'll just go bankrupt.' Until then, we had never suffered any failures, but this pushed us into a financial crisis. It literally changed my life. I was an emotional wreck."

Plunged into despair, Wally was paralyzed with fear realizing he was about to lose it all. He owed people millions of dollars and had no money to pay them.

"I kept looking back on what happened and I blamed myself for being so foolish."

Wally Mah was about to learn another key lesson in life and business. If you are honest and operate with integrity, people will not leave you in a time of crisis. His family, friends, and employees hadn't lost faith in him. They banded together and constructed a plan.

"My Senior VP of Finance, Leo Larson, sat me down and laid it on the line. He said, 'You have the ability to turn this thing around. You have enough talent to do it and lots of support from people. You have to get your head straightened out and focus on your work because that is what's going to get you out of this crisis. Focus on what you do best and I'll take care of dealing with the bills.'"

Mah went back to Saskatoon with a plan to pull North Ridge Development out of financial difficulty. He talked to the suppliers and tradespeople he owed money to.

"We worked for six years to pay everyone back. We took care of the smaller guys first and then paid the bigger companies. When you don't have money, you find out quickly who your friends are."

Mah also owed the bank 2.3 million dollars from the fiasco in Edmonton. As units in the project were sold, payments were made and his financial institution seemed to be fine with the arrangement. The day he made the final payment on another unsecured loan for a project in Saskatoon, the bank called in his operating line. Mah says it was devastating.

"I'm not used to someone telling me one thing and the moment it's to their advantage, they say we're done. I value my integrity more than money and I realized then business is all about relationships.

"Six months later, I found another bank, and we are still with them today. That incident laid out our principal strategy; to make our company become less reliant on banks or other land developers, and to protect our company's future. This strategy eventually made us self-sufficient."

By 1998, Mah and Northridge were in a better financial position. Wally says he reviewed the company from top to bottom and decided he needed a vision for the future.

"I realized I was always dependant on people selling me the land I wanted to develop. I changed my strategy and started acquiring real estate."

Stable and steady were key words for Mah over the next ten years. Then the bottom fell out of the market with the U.S. credit crisis and the collapse of the housing sector. North Ridge Development had eighty-five million dollars in inventory and no one bought a house for six months. Wally coaxed Leo Larson, his former financial executive, out of retirement and gathered all his employees in one room.

"I told them, 'Listen. We have a financial crisis and it's not of our own making. Here is our plan to sustain our operation until it passes. I'm assembling a senior management team and we will manage our cash flow to get through this situation, but right now we're not going to do anything.'"

Wally was right. Not only did he outlast the housing and economic meltdown, he emerged in better financial shape than the competition.

"The following year we were the only company with inventory because everyone had wholesaled themselves out. We chose not to panic. We had another meeting and I received the biggest cheer ever in my life. It reaffirmed our ability to manage. I wouldn't have had the same confidence without the experience in 1992 when we were on the verge of bankruptcy."

Since the events of 2008, North Ridge Development has returned to expansion and profitability. They currently operate in fourteen municipalities throughout Saskatchewan and have acquired stabilized assets, including malls, offices buildings, and warehouses. The North Ridge group of companies is on target to make sales of 250 million this year.

"I have a wonderful wife and family who sacrificed a lot to stay with me over the years. I have an outstanding partner who never lost faith in me. I have loyal employees who care about the company and are still with me today." Wally pauses for a moment, then says, "Colleen and I also make sure we look after our community by donating to numerous charities, the Children's Hospital, and supporting scholarships for doctors so they will stay and practice medicine in Saskatchewan."

Mah's looking to the future and formulating a succession plan. His son works in the Regina office of North Ridge Development and he recently gave him advice we should all take to heart.

"I told my son to work hard. You don't have to be smart, just make sure you outwork the competition and then you will win.

"Business is about taking risks and managing your fear. When I failed in 1992, it was the best thing to ever happen to me. It's not my success, it's my failures that have made me who I am today.

Mah's Money Making Tips

✓ Don't make dreams your master, make dreams your aim.

✓ Be honest and conduct yourself with integrity.

✓ Manage risk.

✓ Be fearless.

✓ Don't forget where you came from.

Make the Ordinary Exceptional

Brian Scudamore
Founder and CEO of 1-800-GOT-JUNK

Moments of brilliance can happen anywhere. Brian Scudamore found his inspiration while waiting for a hamburger in a McDonald's drive-thru lane.

"I was contemplating what I was going to do to pay for college," Brian explains remembering back to 1989. "I didn't finish high school and my dad told me he wasn't going to fund university tuition, so I was under a lot of pressure to make something of myself."

While waiting for his order, Brian looked up and saw a red truck with the words Mark's Hauling written on the side. He watched as a huge mound of rubbish in front of a house was being thrown into the vehicle's back box.

"I looked at it and thought, 'That's my ticket.' I took out $1,000 I had in the bank, spent $753 on an old pickup with plywood side panels, and the rest on flyers and business cards. I had a great uniform and knocked on the doors of houses with piles of junk in the front yard, introduced myself, and offered to haul it away.

"I called my company The Rubbish Boys to sound bigger than it was." Brian pauses for a moment and then says with a laugh, "actually it was Rubbish Boy. As it started to grow, it became my business model."

Scudamore made a $1,700 profit in the first year. It wasn't much but it paid for his commerce and business courses. Three years later Brian found himself at a crossroads. A year short of graduation, he took stock and knew it was time to drop out of school again.

"My dad thought I was absolutely nuts and told me so. He said, 'Listen, this business you're building, that opportunity will always be there. You only have a year left. Finish university.'"

He grows quiet recounting the disappointing conversation with his dad. It made sense. However Brian didn't want to wait any longer. The time to expand the company was now, not a year down the road.

"I knew I could always go back to school so I chose to grow the company and see where it would take me. In 1997, eight years into the venture, we hit a million in revenue. That's when I realized this was a business with the potential to grow in markets outside of Vancouver."

With expansion and franchising on the horizon, Scudamore went back to his place of inspiration, the McDonald's drive-thru.

"I had always been fan of their model. Ray Kroc, McDonald's founder, franchised it and grew it as a global brand. I put together a board of advisors to make smart decisions. We had leaders from business, the military, and the sports world. I knew we could pour our passion and energy into building one big organization, bigger than anyone could build alone. Franchising became the ticket."

Brian studied what worked so well at McDonald's and knew every aspect would have to be systemized. From marketing to the call centre, Scudamore overhauled his operation and started recruiting and hiring.

"The model was a tough one because I switched businesses. I went from junk removal to franchising, and they're very different. I had to learn, understand and support a franchise partner, and make it a successful, people-based conglomerate."

Brian re-named the company 1-800-GOT-JUNK and developed a logo, brand, and image. Then he discovered the all-important phone number was already being used by the Department of Transportation in Idaho.

"I made sixty phone calls to them saying, 'Help me, please! I need this number.' Finally I reached someone in the company and had a feeling the man didn't want me to call anymore. He said, 'Here's the number, now go away!'" Brian laughs, recalling the story, but looking into his eyes you see the fire and drive of a man who doesn't back down easily.

"We took the recipe and began recruiting. Our first candidate was in Toronto, but he used to live in Vancouver. I brought him on-board and asked him to run the lead-off franchise. He became the person others wanted to follow and is doing six million dollars in business today."

1-800-GOT-JUNK wasn't built without trials and challenging moments along the way. Scudamore says there were "a million mistakes," recalling the days of cash flow and payroll problems, plus having to fire friends who didn't have the passion for the company Brian was cultivating. All those experiences proved to be trivial compared to the fallout in 2007. Scudamore recruited a president who was a former high ranking executive at one of the most recognized coffee brands in the world.

"In fourteen months she almost bankrupted us. The recession started and we went into an aggressive growth mode. I came close to losing control of my business because the woman wasn't the right fit. She came from running a multi-billion dollar enterprise, was accustomed to spending money, and had a ton of people driving the industry forward. My company was different and things were close to falling apart."

Scudamore found himself in a dangerous situation, and with the corporation crumbling, he wasn't sure where to find the support to make a change.

"I felt everyone thought the new leader was the right person and I had no one on my side. There were two people internally who believed in me and my vision, and I got her out before losing control. I discovered she was trying to bring in private equity funds."

Regaining command, Scudamore hired a new Chief Operating Officer to lead 1-800-GOT-JUNK.

"I went out and found Erik Church, who has been phenomenal. We share the same vision, goals, culture, and values. He's started to aggressively grow our business the way I knew it could happen."

Now, with the right leader in place, 1-800-GOT-JUNK is once again thriving with 850 trucks on the roads in three countries, and is on track to make $200 million in revenue by 2016. Recently Brian added two new brands: a one-day painting service, and a moving company with twenty-five new owners.

"We've made junk removal exceptional, and taken the ordinary projects of painting and moving to a level of service not seen in this industry. We're very excited about the three brands."

Scudamore may have serious battle scars but courage and execution are on his side. He says the biggest attributes a leader can have are clarity and a clear vision of the future.

"Crystallize a picture in your mind of what your business will look, feel, and act like at a point in the future when no one else around you thinks it will happen. Say, 'I believe in it and I'm going to make it happen.' It sounds simple to envision a positive future but if you lock onto it, you can make anything happen."

Brian has fame, money, and the admiration of his peers because over the years 1-800-GOT-JUNK has been featured on Oprah, Dr. Phil, Hoarders, CNN, and in Fortune magazine. Scudamore's parents are also very proud of their son who didn't follow the traditional route to corporate success.

"I look at every single moment in business as tuition. I may have dropped out of school but there is still life-long learning. Every single thing which has gone wrong has been a lesson, teaching me to get to a much greater place. I don't have bad days. I have fun. Sure, there are *moments* but most days I love what I do and the people that surround me. It comes from having a positive attitude, working hard, and working smart." Brian pauses for a moment and then smiles. "I think making the ordinary exceptional will be our legacy."

Not bad for a guy who went for a cheeseburger and drove away with an idea for a multi-million dollar, international company. That's what I call a Happy Meal.

Scudamore's Success Strategy

✓ Vision: Always have a crystal clear picture, written *and* imagined, of where you're headed.

✓ People: Never, ever, compromise on the quality of personnel you bring into your organization.

✓ Culture: Make engagement with your people a priority so that a positive, healthy culture can grow.

✓ Mentors: Keep a close watch on peers you admire. Ask them for help. Take their best practices.

✓ Conceive, Believe, Achieve: You can't go wrong in business or life taking these three basic steps.

Action is the Key to Success

Bob Dhillon
President and CEO
Mainstreet Equity Corp.

"Mainstreet Equity Corp. was developed from the trunk of my car with a cell phone. Today, I have 1.2 billion dollars worth of assets," Bob Dhillon tells me from his office in downtown Calgary.

Dhillon is a self made man and is on track to become one of the first Sikh billionaires in North America. When you talk to him you discover passion, fire, and boundless energy drive this entrepreneur. Bob is proud of what he has accomplished and of his humble beginnings in Canada.

There are three reasons why I became successful," Bob says with conviction.

"Number one, Canada.
"Number two, Canada.
"Number three, Canada."
Bob pauses for a moment and I realize how serious he is.

"Canada's roads are paved with gold. It grows on trees. It's easy to pluck; you just have to reach for it. I get up every morning and say, 'Thank you Canada.'"

Navjeet (Bob) Singh Dhillon had a unique start in life. His grandfather moved from a Sikh village in India to Hong Kong where he started the North China Shipping Company. Following his lead, Bob's parents became traders in the business.

"My family manufactured goods and products," Dhillon explains. "I was born in Kobe, Japan, and was sent to a private boarding school in India. My parents were at a family outpost in Liberia, West Africa, doing business when there was a coup in the mid-seventies. There was warfare between tribes and, with two young boys, my parents began looking for a country offering safety and security along with long term growth for business people."

Pierre Trudeau was Prime Minister at the time and was encouraging people from other countries to immigrate to Canada.

"Trudeau opened the gates and my parents decided to come to Vancouver."

The move was costly for the Dhillon family and they gave up everything. Bob's parents put their two boys in school, found a place to live, and went to work.

"Sixty thousand Sikhs came to Vancouver, all young, with ambition. It changed the fabric of the city instantaneously," Bob recalls. "It was a very difficult time and it created a recipe for racism."

The Dhillon family moved again, this time to Calgary. Unfortunately, the racism followed when Bob's mother was fired from her job at the post office. They fought back in court and won. She was reinstated a year later, but the treatment they received left a lasting scar. They also arrived in the midst of a very tough recession. Calgary had been booming in the seventies but it all changed with the dawn of a new decade and when the downturn bit hard into the economy. At the age of nineteen, Bob was ready to get a job. Finding the oil and gas industry a "closed shop" he turned to the collapsed real estate market.

"When you're young, you make a lot of gutsy decisions. I bought two boarded up houses for $32,000 a piece. They were in foreclosure and needed a lot of work."

I stop Bob for a moment and ask the $64,000 question. "Where does a nineteen year old find that much money?"

"From a loan shark," Dhillon replies, laughing at the memory. "Actually, he called himself an Equity Lender." Bob chuckles again, remembering the man who gave him his start in business.

"I needed $16,000 for the down payment and I agreed to pay a fee plus eighteen percent interest."

The numbers of the deal were definitely in the Equity Lender's best interest but Dhillon didn't care.

"I was a nineteen year old kid with access to capital. I was set to go."

Bob knew even then he was a marketing and finance guy, not a handyman, so he hired tradespeople to fix the houses. The renovations took about a month.

"There was an old time wheeler-dealer real estate agent named Alex Sherwood. He came to me and said, 'Let me know when you're finished renovating and I'll sell them for you.'

"Sherwood introduced me to a lawyer who did the transaction and when the deal was done, I had made $17,000 profit." Bob pauses for moment and then adds, "Everyone I was connected with in the beginning became a shareholder of my company or stayed with me in some capacity."

"Even the loan shark?" I ask.

"You bet," Bob replies. "He became a big shareholder and my relationship with him continued for the next twenty years until he passed away."

With $17,000 in his pocket, most nineteen year olds might be tempted to buy a fancy car or go on an exotic vacation. Not Bob Dhillon.

"I decided to double my bet," he says. "I went out and bought more houses. I became a merchant in real estate and went into apartments in less than eight months. I flipped every type of real estate from commercial centres to land."

Dhillon put in seventy hour work weeks and was a millionaire by the time he turned twenty-one. Driven by the experience of his family losing everything when they fled from Liberia, he vowed it was never going to happen to him again.

Deciding to expand to other countries, Bob was in Costa Rica exploring opportunities when he became bothered by pains in his lower stomach. Flying back to Calgary, he went through a series of tests and then was shocked when the doctor turned to him and said one word that made his blood run cold.

Cancer. Only in his mid-twenties, Bob was stunned by the diagnosis.

"My cancer doctor told me the treatment was going to kill me but I was going to live. It was an interesting comment and I asked him to explain. He told me, 'The treatment is very harsh. Other chemotherapies prolong life. Your chemotherapy will cure you. It will kill all your cells and only the healthy ones will come back.'"

The months and years following the diagnosis were filled with surgery, pain, and anxiety as Bob endured the gruelling bouts of chemo.

"I lost all my hair, my gums were weak, and I had problems with my teeth. I looked…" Dhillon's voice trails off for a moment and then he says, "I looked dead.

"For days at a time they locked me in a room with pipes sticking in me filled with chemo drugs. It was a killer treatment and it gave me anxiety attacks. It was a real dark time in my life."

With his cell phone as his lifeline in the treatment rooms, Dhillon decided to make a major change to his business plan.

"I stayed in a cash position. I was still a very aggressive real estate merchant, but until I received my clean bill of health I remained a day trader."

Five years later, Dhillon was finally given the news he had worked so hard for. Bob was cancer free.

"The doctor said the chances of the cancer coming back were one percent. Then he said, 'I don't ever want to see you again, forget you met me, forget about the treatment, and move on.'

"I had a new life." Bob pauses for a moment and then regains his energy as he continues. "I did three things. I went back to school and did my MBA at Western. I returned to Costa Rica but realized during my five years of treatment the party was over, and I had missed the market. So, I bought a three thousand acre island in Belize and started laying the foundation for my company going public."

Even while battling cancer, Dhillon had kept his empire growing, buying and selling real estate worth $150 million. With $17 million he started Mainstreet Equity Corp. It was time to move out of the trunk of the car into an office.

Focussing on the mid-sized apartment market, Bob began buying buildings in distress and disrepair. After fixing them, Dhillon was able to rent them out at a profit. Today he owns buildings in Alberta, British Columbia, Saskatchewan, and Ontario and Mainstreet has 1.2 billion dollars in assets. Bob is also developing his land in Belize and is now selling building lots. The land is an exclusive neighbourhood with A-list celebrities such as Leonardo Di Caprio and Madonna owning property around the corner. He even wrote a book about how to invest and retire on the island.

"I'm only beginning my entrepreneurial life. It took me many years to set up a foundation and platform to launch. Now I'm ready and looking forward to going into the U.S. market. Finally, I'm getting capital market recognition."

Dhillon has also been speaking to business students and aspiring young entrepreneurs.

"It's freedom of thought. I tell them to think outside of the box and improvise. Being an entrepreneur is taking risks at the wrong time and fighting against trends. However, the most important piece of information I can give is to not take advice from your friends and family. Only ask successful people.

"I also believe your positive energy has to become your mantra in life. Say this to yourself everyday, 'Yes I can.' You need the right mental attitude. For example, if you have cancer, deal with it. In 2009, the capital market crashed. So instead of licking my wounds I bought back forty percent of our stock. It was at six bucks and now it's over thirty-four dollars. We look brilliant, right? Vision without action is a daydream, and action without a vision is a nightmare. Only action will lead to results."

It's not all work and real estate ventures rounding out Bob Dhillon's life. He will not talk about his family for religious reasons, however, the man is an open book in all other areas. He is a professional salsa dancer, practices yoga daily, and enjoys spear fishing and surfing.

"Money is a great slave and a terrible master. Don't fall in love with it, money is only a vehicle. Fall in love with yourself."

Bob pauses for a moment, reflecting on his journey so far in life and business. He started with nothing, beat a deadly disease, and went on to create one of Canada's most successful companies. I ask for a final thought from the self-made billionaire. Dhillon pauses for a moment then says with fire and conviction, "On the balance sheet of life, people are the most important, not money. For me, that's what this world is all about."

Billionaire Bob's Bullet Points

✓ Learn from your failures. Winners never quit.

✓ Remain positive and practice doing it until it becomes a way of life. It has to be a religion.

✓ Stay in the race when times get tough. No one has ever hit a home run from the stands.

✓ Take advice only from people who are successful in the field you want to get into.

✓ Action plus intelligence will make you a king.

The Golden Age of Entrepreneurship

Terry Beech
Co-Founder and CEO
HiretheWorld, Entrepreneur, and Educator

The trendy restaurant in downtown Vancouver is vibrating with youthful energy and loud, boisterous conversations. Claiming the last two seats, I squeeze into a small space in the packed eatery that caters to university students and young, urban professionals. It's a perfect place to meet Terry Beech and the first time I lay my eyes on the young man striding towards the table I'm stunned at what I see. The successful businessman and entrepreneurship professor must have found the fountain of youth because, at thirty-two years of age, he looks as if he just graduated from school.

I stand to shake his hand, but with a grin breaking out across his face he envelops me in a big bear hug. We have been conversing for months by phone and our friendship has swung into an easy alliance of trust. He's down-to-earth, very approachable, and extremely entertaining. As we talk, one aspect of this young entrepreneur becomes abundantly clear to me. I am convinced there isn't anything Terry Beech can't accomplish.

Growing up in Victoria, Terry learned the value of money early in life. He wore secondhand clothing, his orange juice was diluted with water to make it last longer, hair cuts were done by dad, and there wasn't enough money to take part in hotdog day at school. Terry didn't complain. He says the lack of money at home taught him to be more resourceful.

"My first inclination to be an entrepreneur came when I saw my first Nintendo game," he tells me from across the table. "All the kids were playing it and I asked my mom why we didn't have one. She told me we didn't have any money. So I thought, 'What is this money thing and how can I get some?'"

Terry and his twin brother, Doug, shared three newspaper routes, collected pop bottles, and organized puppet shows, charging people twenty-five cents admission. By the time he was fourteen years old, Beech was a businessman-in-training and he was more than ready when Mother Nature dumped a huge opportunity into his backyard.

"We had a massive blizzard. It was the worst storm ever in Victoria and people's roofs were caving in. The next day, my cousin, brother and I found three shovels and went door-to-door shoveling snow off roofs. It was dangerous, so we tied ourselves to the chimneys with yellow rope and we made thousands and thousands of dollars. It was the first time we had made really big money."

Terry also excelled at school. By grade twelve he not only was a member of the debate team, he was coaching it. With a municipal election on the calendar, Beech decided to run for city council in the seaside city of Nanaimo. The fact he had recently turned eighteen didn't faze him at all. With his debate team agreeing to help run his campaign, Terry knew research and hard work would be the key to winning the election. Beech threw himself into the task, requesting disclosure statements from the city clerk. He researched the actions of every past councillor and analyzed what they had spent money on. Terry met with all city departments, toured maintenance facilities, and studied engineering reports. He spent weeks in the local library going through microfilm of old newspapers, studying all the issues so if someone asked him a question on the campaign trail he would have an opinion.

"They didn't even invite me to the first candidates meeting." Terry recalls. "During the second meeting, I started gaining momentum. I held my ground and people saw I was a serious candidate. I knew the issues, the money started coming in, and we began to roll."

When the ballots were counted on election night, Beech had done it. At eighteen years and four months, he was the youngest politician ever elected in Canada, an honour he holds to this day.

While serving on city council, Beech went to university, studying business and economics. He was an excellent student, graduating in the ninety-ninth percentile with over $100,000 in scholarship money.

Look out world. Beech had landed.

Terry certainly wasn't shy in his approach to the world and business. After winning the Student Impact Award, he knew there was one man he had to meet. Francesco Aquilini of the Aquilini Investment Group was on the Award Selection Committee. Learning he was scheduled to attend the awards dinner, Beech was determined to connect with him that night.

"I arrived early and approached the lady who was organizing the dinner. I asked, 'Can you put my business card in Mr. Aquilini's name tag?' I thought he would find it, then would know who I was when he met me. Later on, I was telling a group of people what I had done but I didn't know Francesco was standing behind me, listening to my story." Terry pauses and laughs at the gaffe, then continues. "I only wanted to have lunch with him, however, he had other ideas. We got along famously, and he hired me right away to come work with him. I remember he told me that if I wanted to be entrepreneurial, I'd have every chance to do so at his company. It was like getting ten MBA's in two-and-a-half years. The amount of learning, opportunities, negotiations, and knowledge I gained while working with him was invaluable."

On a steep learning curve, Beech plunged into the next challenge and decided to get his MBA. Accepted at one of the top business schools in the world, Terry left Canada for England, enrolling at Oxford to focus on entrepreneurship and finance.

"I had a meeting with two career counselors my first week at Oxford. I told them I didn't want a career; I wanted to become an entrepreneur. They didn't understand."

Beech entered a venture capital competition where close to sixty MBA programs from around the world were competing against each other. They won the European finals and were invited to the World Championships. Beech and his MBA team from Oxford didn't win, but they made history. No European team or one year MBA program had ever placed at the World's, but they did, with their second place finish.

With a prestigious accomplishment on his resume and his Oxford MBA completed, Terry made plans to return to Canada. It was 2009, and he was in serious debt due to his tuition and the stock market crash the year before. It was decision time. Would he work for a corporation and make $200,000 a year or start his own business?

Terry weighed his options and thought about a new venture he had recently learned about called crowd sourcing. The internet had made the world a level playing field and geography no longer played a role in working together. People from all over the world could come together on a project with the click of a mouse.

"I called my brother and convinced him to work with me. I had already mocked up my own website for a logo design company and that was the beginning of HiretheWorld. Neither of us is technical, so we brought in a programmer and made Arash Afrooze the third founding partner. We sourced online communities, finding five hundred graphic designers from forty countries willing to work with us. We found a company and submitted the first design brief. Staring at the computer, we were saying, 'please-please-please, somebody, someone design something!' It took twenty-four hours for the first design to come in but by the end of the contest the company had over one hundred designs to choose from."

HiretheWorld, a logo, website and graphic design company, launched in June of 2009 and they mapped out a plan to make money in the first 120 days. Looking for other ways to create revenue, they decided to go after venture funding to grow their business.

"We pitched to everybody and applied for a couple of competitions. We beat out 160 finalists to win the New Venture, B.C. competition and received a $123,000 prize package. We also closed a seed funding round of about $500,000 with a group of investors. However, it wasn't all roses. We pitched to a lot of angel investors and venture capitalists and got more no's than yes's."

Beech and his partners went into expansion mode and immediately made a big mistake. Looking for other ways to use crowd sourcing they expanded into videos, text, and translation.

"We had a lack of focus and were in the middle of situations we didn't want to be in. In one case, Spanish text wasn't translated correctly and we spent too much time trying to fix things. Our design revenue started declining and we were incurring a lot of extra costs to service the 570 categories we had branched into. We looked at the numbers and realized we'd be much better off if we shut down the extra categories and focused on the design work."

As soon as Beech and his partners fixed the problem they went on to produce record profits every month. In 2012, they were named one of the twenty most innovative companies in British Columbia. Terry has since gone on to found Beech Partners and is currently helping grow four new start-ups.

As passionate as Terry is about being in business he's also become a huge advocate of expanding entrepreneurial education. He is a passionate and sought-out speaker on the subject and keynotes regularly at events such at the National Innovation Awards, and even recently joined multi-millionaire entrepreneur Robert Herjavec from The Dragon's Den and Shark Tank at an event to help small business owners grow their businesses. As an adjunct professor of entrepreneurship at two universities, Terry continues to teach strategy and finance to the next generation of entrepreneurs.

"I've been teaching in the undergraduate department at Simon Fraser University for the last five years and have been working hard to get entrepreneurship taught outside of just the business school. I'm also teaching at UBC in a masters program that is designed exclusively for non-business majors. Canada is unique in the world in that we invest very heavily in research and development, but rank poorly in terms of innovation and commercialization. I think we can change this by arming our youth with an entrepreneurial education and mindset. A few years ago as an Action Canada Fellow, I got together with a group of leaders from across the country and we examined this issue very closely. In drafting a strategy for High Growth Entrepreneurship in Canada, we discovered that broadening entrepreneurial education could have massive quality of life benefits for all Canadians. Over ninety percent of all new jobs are derived from high-growth companies, and it's our job to empower our population with the skills to build these companies. This is why I've positioned myself as a key player in curriculum development and advocacy, because I think it's critical to arm our population with an entrepreneurial toolset."

What has Terry discovered?

"One of the biggest problems I see is people thinking they know what they want, yet by the time they get it, realizing it's not what they were aiming for in the first place. You have to understand yourself and find out what drives you. Once you know that, you can start building something that you will truly value and appreciate. Even now, I still find myself giving my head a shake and questioning my decisions, so it is an ongoing process.

"Focus is also important because there are a lot of distractions. If you don't know where you're heading, other people will focus your attention for you. However, if you know what you want, you have a ten times better chance getting it. Never be afraid to ask yourself the question, 'Am I doing this for me or for someone else?'"

Beech says now is the time to start a company because we are living in the golden age of entrepreneurship.

"It's an exciting time for entrepreneurship. Online commerce in particular is currently in the state of a perpetual gold rush. We're pioneering, there are no rules, and no one has figured everything out yet. With technology evolving as fast as it is, there is still unlimited opportunity. The cost of starting a business or reaching a global market has never been lower. If you can figure out who your customer is and zero in on them then the world is your oyster. That's why entrepreneurship is so great. The cost of entry and the risk associated with it is at all time record lows and the potential payoff is at record highs."

It's not all work and business for Terry. He recently married, likes to travel the world, and is considering making a run at Parliament Hill in Ottawa.

"I'm definitely excited about getting involved in politics. In the meantime, there are several start-ups I have invested in and I'm also getting into real estate."

He's also giving back by being involved in LIFT, Canada's largest venture philanthropy organization which provides the resources and knowledge for non-profit companies to scale their organizations and improve their social impact. Terry also is passionate about the non-profit he and Doug created eight years ago. Twinbro facilitates getting relatable role models into classrooms at a critical turning point in a student's life. The organization inspires youth to seek out a higher education, and also shows them how to win scholarships in order to fund their tuition.

"We've held seminars for thirty-five thousand students across Canada and the U.S. They've gone on to win millions in scholarships," Terry tells me excitedly. "Several students have won over $100,000 on their own."

Terry grows reflective as our time together draws to a close.

"You know, it's been a wild ride and at the age of thirty-two I feel as if I've lived ten lifetimes."

I look at Terry in awe. He's so young and has accomplished much in life. Yet Beech doesn't want admiration, he's too busy looking for the next opportunity.

"I understand how hard it is to make money. However, I feel that if you focus not on the money, but on creating exceptional value for your customers, wealth will surely follow.

"I will continue to launch businesses and I will definitely continue to work as an educator. I've taught thousands of students and helped their businesses grow. It's been a really satisfying experience for me."

Terry overcame poverty to find success because he refused to be defined or labeled in this world. He is a shining example of how it's not where you start out in life, it is how you finish.

Beech's Building Blocks for Business

✓ Time is your most valuable resource.

✓ Have an intense focus on value creation. Think about how you can make a person's life better rather than make another dollar. If you can identify and solve a really painful problem for your customer then the money will eventually come.

✓ Surround yourself with amazing people who love what they do. Being an entrepreneur is hard enough and you don't need to waste your time and energy with employees or partners who are only adequate. If you want to be a rock star, surround yourself with the same and your odds of success will exponentially increase.

✓ Do not fear what other people think of you as it will prevent you from taking appropriate risks. Crisis is usually temporary, but the regret from not pursuing an opportunity can last a lifetime.

✓ Have fun. Life is too short and too amazing to leave happiness for non-business hours only.

Tools and Strategies Every Entrepreneur Needs to Know

Terry Beech

From Inspiration to Entrepreneur ❋

Canada needs more entrepreneurs.

When Teresa first contacted me about this book, I was energized by the opportunity to persuade more Canadians to start their own business. While everyone loves a good rags-to-riches story, there are few who care to venture beyond the safety of nine-to-five employment. Our risk avoiding culture tends to prefer the comfort of a limited but sustaining paycheque over the pursuit of a greater, but unknown, future.

Despite the accolades often associated with a successful entrepreneur, the profession does not "stick" as a realistic or celebrated career option. Ask a child what she wants to be when she grows up and "An Entrepreneur" almost never makes the list. Given the lack of exposure the average Canadian has to the subject, this is hardly surprising. Entrepreneurship, or even business in general, is not a part of the K-12 curriculum. There are a few courageous courses in some high schools labeled "Entrepreneurship" but little beyond that. Universities haven't fared much better, as entrepreneurship programs have only recently begun to find their place.

What Canadian universities have traditionally been quite good at is preparing our students to be excellent employees or academic researchers. We have fallen short, however, in preparing our students to be excellent entrepreneurs. High growth companies are built from innovative and disruptive technologies and they account for over 90% of our economy's net new jobs. As a society, Canada contributes more to research and development per capita than any other nation on earth[1]. Despite this contribution, we continue to rank very low in terms of innovation and commercialization. This means that while Canadians are quite good at creating new and exciting ideas and technologies, we don't translate this success into new job-creating enterprises.

Solving the innovation and commercialization deficit is easily one of Canada's greatest economic opportunities. Finding ways to bolster the development and growth of Canadian enterprises will be a linchpin in securing Canada's long-term prosperity. Fortunately for all of us, there is hope. We happen to be living in the golden age of entrepreneurship. Others may not have recognized it, but it's changing the dynamics of the Canadian workforce and the way many choose to live.

This increase in entrepreneurial activity is no accident. Traditional job security continues to erode. Income inequality continues to expand. Average incomes of the middle class have maintained a gradual yet steady decline as families struggle to keep pace with price increases. These factors work to lower the perceived risk of becoming an entrepreneur. Combine this with unprecedented access to capital, labour, and global markets and you have the foundation for an entrepreneurial gold rush.

Who are these new entrepreneurs? They are doctors, lawyers, high school drop-outs, and inventors; they are teachers and tech gurus and social activists. They are all around us and their numbers are growing every day. Demand for entrepreneurial education is growing faster globally than any other subject. In 2013, Britain's enterprise advisor to the Prime Minister advocated that every single undergraduate student in the UK be given some form of entrepreneurial education prior to graduating. In most western economies, governments are investing billions in the hope of creating a more entrepreneurial society. We are witnessing what is essentially an innovator's arms race.

In the next three chapters, I will not only convince you that entrepreneurship is a viable and worthwhile career option, but I'll give you some tools to help get you started. To match the thirty inspirational stories, I will provide thirty

---

[1] Beech et al. (2011). Global Gazelles: A National Strategy for High Growth Entrepreneurship in Canada. Available: http://www.actioncanada.ca/en/pdf/FuellingCanadasEconomicSuccess-ANationalStrategyForHigh-GrowthEntrepreneurship.pdf. Last accessed 20th October, 2013.

pieces of entrepreneurial insight and advice. In the first chapter I'll offer ten reasons WHY you should become an entrepreneur. In the second chapter I'll show you HOW to think like an entrepreneur. In the third chapter I'll show you WHERE to find the resources you need to get started. I will do this by telling you the story of HiretheWorld, a company I co-founded and built from scratch.

If this sounds interesting to you, and you have been inspired by the other stories in this book, then I invite you to read the next three chapters with earnest. We are living in a global marketplace where half the world is only a few clicks away. If you've ever told someone, "I'd like to have my own business one day," then there has been no better time to pursue your dream. My hope is that the tools provided here will inspire you to turn your entrepreneurial ideas into action.

I want you to be an entrepreneur.

Ten Reasons Why You
Should be an Entrepreneur

Entrepreneurs are agents of change. They create, renew, improve, and invigorate. In driving things forward entrepreneurs create opportunity. Schumpeter, the Austrian-American economist, labelled this force "creative destruction." Entrepreneurship can empower an individual, lower societal constraints, and enable a life of passion and creativity. Our quality of life is dependent on this change. In fact, we are so dependent on the forces of innovation that one could argue there is a moral obligation for a society to arm its citizenry with the entrepreneurial knowledge and tools required to make this change possible.

Entrepreneurial education should begin in elementary school, alongside mathematics and other foundational studies. It should continue throughout high school and be included in university, independent of whether you are a business major, a scientist, or a philosopher. If such an educational policy were adopted, it would unlock an immeasurable amount of potential that would benefit any society that undertook it.

For now, however, society will have to wait. I will work on convincing you, the reader, that it is in your best interest to become an entrepreneur.

What is Entrepreneurship?

The best definition of entrepreneurship I have encountered was defined by Howard Stevenson, a Professor of the subject at Harvard University. The definition reads as follows:

"Entrepreneurship is the pursuit of opportunity without regard to resources currently controlled."

I like this definition for two reasons. The first is that it defines the subject in a way that does not limit an entrepreneur's potential. There is no specific goal or achievement, just the unconstrained pursuit of an opportunity. The second reason is that it excludes the mention of business, a subject with which entrepreneurship is usually associated. This means that entrepreneurship applies just as much to an artist or an Olympic athlete as it does to a restaurateur or a CEO.

In fact, almost any significant achievement has almost certainly relied on some form of entrepreneurship. Michael Phelps did not receive eighteen Olympic gold medals simply because he was a good swimmer. He had to hustle to find facilities, coaches, airplane tickets, food, and professional nutrition consultations. You can bet that Michael spent more time accumulating resources and investment than most business entrepreneurs. He had to sell himself and his goals to endless parents, teachers, coaches, and eventually, governments and corporations. It is the same story that has played out countless times over every generation. Entrepreneurship and its skills are the founding principles of any major achievement. It is not something you are born with. It is something that is developed over time with practice, knowledge, and exposure, just like Michael Phelp's strong butterfly stroke.

Types of Entrepreneurs: Finding Where You Fit

In business, entrepreneurs come in all shapes and sizes. They are tech geeks, treasure hunters, dog walkers, and corner store operators. The kind of entrepreneur you would like to be has everything to do with the reasons for becoming an entrepreneur in the first place. There are a few stereotypical types of entrepreneurs and it's good to know where you might fit.

The Passion Junkies: Many people become entrepreneurs because they want to spend their life doing something that they enjoy. Entrepreneurship, for them, is about finding a way to make a living while doing what you enjoy. This is one of the best reasons to become an entrepreneur. Entrepreneurs who only work on things that they are passionate about are incredibly happy individuals, and generally live very fulfilling lives. A spin-off benefit of this approach is that passionate individuals also tend to spend more time working in their field than their non-passionate counterparts. This investment of time and energy generally makes them experts in their craft and propels them to the top income brackets of their profession. This is why many seasoned individuals preach that you should follow your passion and that the money will surely follow. The missing piece is that it is entrepreneurship that allows you to get there.

The World Changers: Not completely independent of the passion junkies are the world changers. These individuals generally have a higher calling to make an impact on the world around them. They see difficult problems as opportunities, and are highly motivated to seek out new, innovative solutions. Elon Musk, founder of Tesla, SpaceX, and the proposed Hyperloop is an excellent example of a world changing entrepreneur. People often state their opinion of something they think should be changed, followed by a few lines of defeat such as "But what can I do? I am only one person." Ironically, it is usually the single entrepreneur who invokes great change in the world, not the masses. If you have a cause or a vision of something you think should be changed in the world, then an entrepreneurial approach is almost always the path forward.

The Be-Your-Own-Boss: Many people become entrepreneurs simply to avoid being constrained by the traditional workplace. Some don't like reporting to a supervisor or manager, others don't like to be dependent on a single organization for their well-being. When you join a corporation as an employee, you are expected to fulfil your duties within a certain set of specified constraints that has been determined by someone else in advance of your arrival. This is because corporations become more consistent and standardized over time, with little room for large deviations from the standard normal. While standardization can be a useful tool for consistency and flow, it can be mind-numbingly constraining to an individual's personal creativity. These systems can also run counter to how you prefer to live your life. The nine-to-five grind is a great system for many, but a prison for others, and entrepreneurship is often a way out. Advances in technology have allowed individuals to become more empowered, and many new age entrepreneurs work when they want, how they want, from where they want.

The Wealth Creators: Although not the best reason, financial wealth is certainly one of the most cited reasons for becoming an entrepreneur. As I will discuss later in this chapter, modern western society is designed specifically with the entrepreneur in mind. Everything from government grants, to tax policy, to the governing laws of the land are designed to benefit the entrepreneur. Facilitating the birth of high growth enterprises has become the holy grail of government economic policy, and there is a global race to provide the world's most competitive ecosystem to conduct business. The spin-off benefit of these policies is that the entrepreneur has been given a legislative advantage and, as a result, they are amongst the richest individuals in almost every western democracy on the planet.

Although many entrepreneurs fall into at least one of these four general categories, the fact is that entrepreneurs come in all shapes and sizes. Since entrepreneurs make their own rules and define their own success, it would be futile to try to label all of the entrepreneurs of the world. It is indisputable, however, that all entrepreneurs enjoy a unique set of benefits and perks that are not available to the average employee. In the remainder of this chapter I am going to articulate ten of these benefits to further persuade you to become an entrepreneur.

Reason #1 - The Golden Age of Entrepreneurship is Now

There has been no better time to start a business. Technology has reduced start-up costs to record lows while the rewards of succeeding have skyrocketed to all time highs. The internet is facilitating free access to information, communication, and customers. There is an abundance of investment capital available and there is a growing social acceptance of entrepreneurship as a viable and noble career path. There is a virtual gold rush occurring around the world, and it's the entrepreneur's pan in the river.

At the same time, the alternative of traditional employment is becoming less attractive. Job security has eroded, and benefits like pension plans and healthcare are no longer guaranteed. In addition, the changing landscape of the global economy and the speed of technological innovation are disrupting and destroying traditional careers. The best path forward is no longer a forty year commitment to a single company. The new economy requires an adaptive strategy, an evolutionary trajectory, and an entrepreneurial approach.

Reason #2 - Being an Entrepreneur is an Amazing Life Skill

We defined entrepreneurship as the pursuit of opportunity without regard for resources, so it doesn't necessarily mean that you need to quit your job to be an entrepreneur. Embracing the mindset of an entrepreneur can improve your life without having to actually run your own business. Treating entrepreneurship as a life skill means determining what your goals are and then finding unique ways to accomplish them. Focus on tapping into your creativity, look for opportunities, and don't be shy about challenging the status quo.

Have you ever negotiated a deal at a retail store like Walmart? No? Why not? Most individuals pay whatever the price is that is listed on the shelf, with no idea that they may not have to. My office chair retails for $250, but I purchased it for $75 because it was the show model and it had some chalk on the back of it. It was $75 because, as an entrepreneur, I saw an opportunity to challenge the status quo and get what I wanted for significantly less cash. Whereas others might have been happy paying the $250, I asked for a discount, and got it. Now I have an additional $175 to put towards my next project or adventure.

In a similar vein, I have a friend who lives in an amazing two-storey penthouse in downtown Vancouver. The home is worth about two million dollars and my friend's income doesn't even come close to paying the mortgage. But you know what? My friend wanted a two-storey penthouse in Vancouver, so he put on his entrepreneurial hat, and figured out a non-traditional way of getting what he wanted. The main living area is huge and has an amazing view of the city, so he leases it out for private parties. Not only do these events cover his mortgage, but they put some extra money in his pocket as well. In addition, he gets to live his dream of living in an impressive two-storey penthouse in one of the world's most expensive real estate markets. My friend doesn't own a business per se, he still works a full-time job, but let's face it, he's a very successful entrepreneur.

Every day there are opportunities to be an entrepreneur popping up all around you. Entrepreneurs don't go through a typical day letting stuff happen to them, they make stuff happen for them. The more practice you have at challenging the status quo, the more you realize that rules are bendable in most situations and completely rewritable in others. As you gain more experience in this, you gain more confidence. As you gain more confidence, more opportunities arise. We refer to that as a virtuous cycle.

An entrepreneur's confidence is what helps them sell themselves and their ideas to other people. I find most successful entrepreneurs combine this skill with a heightened sense of humility. On one hand they are strong enough to sell an idea, but humble enough to ask for help. I first observed this in myself when I ran for public office. On one hand, I needed to convince a city that I was the best man for the job (sales), and on the other hand, I spent over a year researching and recruiting the help of others (humility). These entrepreneurial skills have helped me in all kinds of situations, both inside and outside the boardroom. It's how I became Canada's youngest politician, it's how my friend bought his dream condo, and it's how you can accomplish your goals as well.

Reason #3 - Freedom + Independence = Opportunity

Ever notice that your best opportunities always seem to conflict with work? Your best friend gets front row tickets but you have to work overtime, or maybe you were invited to spend a week at the cabin but had already used up your vacation time. North American working culture starts you at two measly weeks of vacation per year. This is an incredibly small amount of time. If you assume that you take at least one week for Christmas, you are almost completely locked into hanging around your office or cubicle for most of the year.

The worst part about being chained to an office isn't the opportunities that you miss, it's the opportunities you'll never hear about. Human beings are creatures of habit and once you are into a routine, people around you will adjust to accommodate. If a friend offered you a stay at their cabin for the last two years and you turned it down both times, then it's likely that your friend will just stop inviting you. Employment opportunities work the same way. Once you settle into a job, the opportunities come by less often. Not only are you "off the radar" to people looking for your skills, you are also less open to seeking new opportunities. Entrepreneurs are always open to new opportunities, and therefore individuals continue to bring them forward. Most entrepreneurs have more interesting projects on their plate than they can take on at any one time. Now that's job security!

The other benefit of being an entrepreneur is that you get more control in setting your schedule. This means you don't necessarily need to operate on the socially acceptable time of Monday to Friday from 9am to 5pm. For example, my brother, Doug, who is also an entrepreneur, regularly makes Tuesday his Saturday. This means that when he goes skiing he's the only one on the mountain and when he goes to the bank he doesn't have to stand in line. He can get in twice the number of ski runs and do twice the amount of chores on Tuesday, and then make up his work on Saturday when the mountain and the bank are packed. Operating outside of "standard social time" also has great monetary benefits. Vacation planning is a great example of this, as you can usually save up to 50% by travelling during off peak times. This means that every time you go on vacation as an entrepreneur you've saved enough to go on your next one.

Reason #4 - It's Ten Times Easier to Become Wealthy

I would never recommend becoming an entrepreneur for the money, but if you want to make real money, entrepreneurship is the way to go. At university I studied business and economics. In business we regularly studied successful entrepreneurs. Scroll through the Forbes list of billionaires and you will stumble across a plethora of entrepreneurs (or heirs of entrepreneurs).

In economics I focused on developmental economics, or the economics of how nations build wealth. The longer you study economics the more you realize how little we know about how the economy actually works. It's kind of like studying the brain; we have the general principles of what levers control what, but the system itself is too complicated to completely map out. Despite this, one outcome consistently emerged in every single model I studied. It was always the owner and never the worker who ended up on top.

I did some research and tried to figure out if I could find some working professionals who became billionaires. The closest I could find was Roberto Goizueta of Coca Cola. This legendary CEO actually started at a bottling company in Cuba prior to defecting to the United States. After forty-three years of hard work with the organization, he became the first billionaire manager. To accomplish this he had to expand Coca Cola globally, and increase the value of the company by over 7100 percent. By the time Roberto was worth a billion dollars, Coke achieved a market capitalization of almost $180 billion. Jack Welch, General Electric's prolific CEO, was also at the helm for over forty years and increased the value of his company from $14 billion dollars to over $484 billion. Despite this, Jack never quite made it to billionaire status.

Although each of these individuals was incredibly entrepreneurial and enjoyed enormous success, their share of wealth was relatively dismal compared to the value they helped create within their organizations. Mr. Goizueta didn't become a billionaire because he was paid a large salary. He became a billionaire because he had a large ownership stake in the business he was heading.

If you want to make a million dollars a year as an employee, you need to figure out how to make your company at least ten million. I call this the rule of ten. It's a hard mission to accomplish, and it's an even harder mission to sustain. Once a corporation has essentially learned how you made them ten million dollars, the company will actively seek out ways to lower your income. As an employee, you are an expense to your organization and represent a drain on shareholder value. As an owner, you are aligned with the goals of management and the organization, which is to increase the value of the company as much as possible. Entrepreneurs find themselves on the shareholder side of the equation more often. This is why they dominate the Forbes list. So if you want to be really wealthy, become an entrepreneur.

Reason #5 - You Don't Have the Time to Do It Later

Many people want to start their own business, but expect it to happen sometime in the future. There are always reasons and distractions to prevent you from getting started. Many feel that you can always get to it later. The problem is most people never get to it. It's not because they're lazy or have a lack of ambition. In most cases it's just a mathematical impossibility.

In his book *Outliers*, Malcolm Gladwell postulates that it takes approximately 10,000 hours to be an expert at anything. This means that if you want to be a really good piano player or build a really great business, you can expect to invest around 10,000 hours or more into the endeavour. Most people don't do the math to figure out exactly how much time they've got to take on these activities. Fortunately, I've done some of the math for you:

Let's start by making some basic assumptions about what takes up time in the average person's life. I assume that we write off the first five years to the development of basic language and motor skills. We follow this up by approximately seventeen years of education and socialization as an individual learns about the world and discovers who they are. I assume that each of us gets eight hours of sleep per night and that two-and-a-half hours are dedicated to either eating or hygiene. On average, we travel approximately an hour a day, and I've dedicated three hours to general entertainment, watching television, or other individual routines or habits.

Average Activities:	Time Commitment:
Basic Language and Motor Skills	5 Years
Standard K-12 plus Some Post-Secondary	17 Years
Average Amount of Sleep Needed per Day	8 Hours per day = 24 Years
Daily Commute / Travel Time	1 Hour per day = 3 Years
Socializing and Entertainment	3 Hours per day = 9 Years
Eating and Hygiene	2.5 Hours per day = 7 Years
Total Allocated Time:	**569,400 Hours or 65 Years**

When you add up all of these life activities, you really only have the opportunity to be an expert in ten things in your life. Of course this doesn't take into account the time most will spend in a typical forty year career. Taking this additional 80,000 hours into account, you really only have time to be an expert in two things. Add kids or a serious medical issue into that equation, and you've simply run out of time.

Calculating Personal Creative Time:	Time Commitment:
Total Allocated Time:	**569,400 Hours or 65 Years**
Remaining Time for Creative Endeavours:	105,120 Hours = 10 Expert Activities
Subtract the Average 9-5 Job for Forty Years	- 80,000 Hours
Personal Creative Time with a 9-5 Job:	25,120 Hours = 2 Expert Activities

I think it's interesting if you examine the life of someone who has had a brush with death, or some other form of life crisis. It's almost as if they woke up and realized that life was passing them by. If you're not doing what you want to do, if you're not building what you want to build, then you need to know that time is running out. If you want to accomplish something or be something in the future, your crisis should be that you're not currently working on that goal right now. Most people don't get started because they are afraid of something, usually the possibility of failure or change. People who go through a crisis tend to lose this fear, and begin to approach things head on. Remind yourself that action is the best cure for fear, and that entrepreneurs are the most impatient, action oriented, and fearless individuals you will ever meet.

Reason #6 - The Tax System Punishes Employees and Rewards Entrepreneurs

I was twenty-five when I negotiated my first six-figure salary. I had worked really hard to attain this achievement and I was very happy the day that I attained it. I could hardly wait for two weeks to go by so that I could see that first deposit in my account. When the money finally arrived I logged into my bank account and was disappointed by what I saw. I had risen through a couple of tax brackets that year, and couldn't believe the size of my income tax deduction. A stern realization washed over me, the fact that over forty cents of every dollar I earned was no longer mine. It's a shocking truth that for most of us, taxes, and not our home, will be the single largest expense of our lifetime.

As an employee there are almost no tax benefits to take advantage of. You can't write off your expenses, and most of your deductions are mandated by law. This means that your taxes become a way of life, and simply a necessary burden that most are willing to bear.

Entrepreneurs also have to pay taxes, but are granted many benefits that employees simply don't have access too. First of all, corporate income taxes are always lower than personal income taxes. This is due to the fact that a corporation's employees will also pay tax, resulting in double taxation. However, a corporation's owners don't necessarily have to distribute a company's wealth through traditional employment wages. An entrepreneur can also earn their income through dividends or capital gains. Each of these has significantly lower rates of taxation and many sizable exemptions which work to keep an entrepreneur's total tax bill down.

Corporations and sole proprietors also have a large opportunity for write offs and exemptions that are not available to employees. Remember the $250 office chair from Walmart? Let's go back and re-examine the purchase of a similar $250 chair in the eyes of both an employee and a small business owner. Let's assume that the marginal income tax rate is 35%, the corporate tax rate is 15%, and the sales tax rate is 10%.

An employee's purchases are always made with after-tax income. This means an employee has to earn significantly more than $250 in order to make a $250 purchase. Given our assumptions, a $250 chair would require an employee to earn an income of $423.08 in order to purchase the chair. This $423.08 would then be taxed at 35% reducing the employee's spending money to $275, which is just enough to cover the cost of the chair ($250) and the sales tax ($25).

A small business owner's purchases are treated as expenses which are then written off against revenues. Sales tax paid on business expenses can also normally be reclaimed against sales tax collected from customers. A sole proprietor would therefore be able to "write off" the chair and reduce their income tax burden by $250*35% or $87.50, effectively reducing the chair's cost to $162.50. A corporation would also be able to reduce their corporate tax burden by $250*15% or $37.50, effectively reducing the chair's cost to $212.50.

	Employee	Sole Proprietor	Corporation
Retail Price	$250	$250	$250
Sales Tax	$25	0 (Reclaimed)	0 (Reclaimed)
Write Off Benefit	0	$87.50 (35%)	$37.50 (15%)
Pre-Tax Income Required	$275/(1.35%) = $423.08	NA	NA
Effective Price	**$423.08**	**$162.50**	**$212.50**

While this example simplifies the tax burden of small businesses by ignoring the initial source of capital, it does a good job of demonstrating some of the tax benefits available to entrepreneurs. In each case, the small business owner can acquire the chair at a significantly cheaper effective rate than an average employee can.

Corporations are also given access to a wide variety of government subsidies, tax credits, and grants. For example, Canada operates the world's largest per capita research and development programs which distribute billions of dollars every year. These funds are generated through taxation, and then funnelled to entrepreneurs and corporations in order to promote innovation, commercialization, and job creation. While the program itself definitely provides a net benefit to all citizens of Canada, it is still an obvious flow of capital from the country's employees to its entrepreneurs.

Reason #7 - The Faster Things Change, the Better

We live in a time of extraordinary change. Technology has made communication and connectedness free and instantaneous. New trends are adopted globally at record speed. A new fashion trend can emerge from Brazil at the same time that a new dance sensation emerges from Korea.

The difference in how we live and how we interact with each other has changed more in the last twenty years than it has in the last hundred. It has been said that nobody likes change. Most entrepreneurs would beg to differ. Disruption of one industry means the emergence of another, and entrepreneurs are the leaders and the benefactors of these Darwinian tidal waves. Where an employee sees change as a problem because they could be at risk of losing their job, an entrepreneur sees change as an opportunity to find a new way to create and capture value.

Reason #8 - You Can Pursue Your Passion

The day you begin working on something you are passionate about is the day that you stop working. When I was in university I told everybody that I planned to retire at the age of thirty. Everyone who knew me thought that there was no way this was going to happen. Not because I wasn't capable of doing it, but because I was incapable of not working.

The truth was that I never meant that I was going to stop working. My definition of retirement was that I would only stop working on things that I wasn't passionate about. I came from a poor background, so I took a lot of jobs that I didn't like when I was growing up. It was the classic exchange of labour for money so I could pursue things that I wanted when I wasn't working. My definition of retirement didn't mean that I wasn't going to make money or stop working on things. It just meant I wasn't going to blindly exchange my labour for money any longer.

Now I only work on things that I am passionate about, and that are fun and fulfilling for me personally. I wake up every morning excited to take on the day and am always motivated to get started. I realized if I wasn't going to go out and live my dream, I was going to spend the rest of my life building someone else's. So I invested my first thirty years into making sure that I would be able to spend all of my time pursuing my passions and my goals. I don't work anymore, I live, and it's made me a happier and wealthier person in the process. The combination of entrepreneurship and education made it possible.

Reason #9 - If You Cheat, You Only Cheat Yourself

One of the worst things about the traditional work force is that employees, in general, are still paid based on attendance instead of performance. This creates some very interesting and painful situations. A friend of mine was recently hired at a government job, replacing someone who had worked in the same position for thirty years. My friend diligently got to work and did her best to be as productive as possible. She was so productive, in fact, that she figured out how to accomplish all of her responsibilities in less than six hours a week. She went to her manager to look for more responsibility but was told to just stick to her job description.

So what's the problem? The problem is she can't just show up on Monday, polish off her responsibilities in six hours, and then go do something else. That would be unacceptable in her work environment. Instead, she has to get through another thirty-four hours of attendance in order to get paid.

Entrepreneurs don't have this problem. We are incentivized to organize our time to be as productive as possible. If you can get your job done in six hours, then you have thirty-four full hours of new time to enjoy or invest in something else. At the same time, if you know you aren't feeling productive, you can spend a couple of hours at the golf course to refocus, and no one will ever complain. You can come back guilt free and get back to work once you are back in your zone.

It's easy to be busy but it's an accomplishment to be productive. As an entrepreneur you have the power to live your life in a more productive state. If you are wasting time, you are not hurting your employer, you are only really cheating yourself. This alignment of incentives means that over time, you will create more value as an entrepreneur than as an employee, and eventually you will be rewarded for it.

Reason #10 - Entrepreneurs Make the Best Employees

Even if the first nine reasons haven't persuaded you to become an entrepreneur, I have a small hedge, which is that you can always become an intrapreneur. An intrapreneur is an individual who takes an entrepreneurial approach to their job or career. I got my first opportunity to be an intrapreneur working at the Aquilini Investment Group. Under the mentorship of one of the group's managing partners, I was given leeway to make decisions, take risks, and most importantly, take ownership of all my projects.

In the three years I worked at the company, I tripled my salary, was regularly promoted, and was given an ever expanding portfolio of projects to work on. I internalized the work and treated the company as if it was my own. This changed how I perceived every problem in the organization. When trouble struck the company on a deal, I would lose just as much sleep as the owners would. This level of care and appreciation didn't go unnoticed, and it created even more opportunities for me.

The fact is that entrepreneurs within organizations make more money, get more opportunities, and are promoted faster than employees who treat their position as just another job. Working in this way is also a great way to gain entrepreneurial experience while still working with someone else's money. This approach takes away much of the risk of being a traditional entrepreneur and, hence, much of the reward. However, it absolutely ensures that you'll have a more fulfilling experience every day that you're on the job.

The Bottom Line

Today there are more reasons than ever to become an entrepreneur. Whether you need more time, more money, or just more freedom, entrepreneurship has a potential answer for you. If the previous ten reasons to become an entrepreneur have intrigued you, than I encourage you to carry on to the next chapter where we will show you HOW to make it happen with ten ways to think and act like an entrepreneur.

Ten Tips to Think and Act Like an Entrepreneur

Entrepreneurs come in all shapes and sizes. While there is no typical entrepreneur, there are some common traits shared among many of the most successful. The following ten tips will help you think and act like an entrepreneur and give you a head start on your next entrepreneurial project.

Tip #1 - Know Why

One of the best ways to become a successful entrepreneur is to understand exactly what you wish to achieve. When you understand what you really want, it is much easier to find the energy to work hard and achieve it. As an example, most people spend their time chasing money, but that pursuit is often misdirected. Nobody wants the actual "money." Instead, they want what the money can buy. This could be a material object, but more often it is the time and freedom to pursue an experience or achieve a higher goal. Many people spend so much time focused on the money that they actually forget why they're chasing it in the first place.

Reflect, take time for yourself, be brutally honest when you look in the mirror, and ask the following questions:

- What is your definition of success?
- What would make you happy?
- What do you actually want to spend your life doing?

Our consumer-based culture has conditioned many people to want "things" like expensive jeans, luxury cars, and impressive jewellery. Unfortunately, most of these things don't actually go very far in increasing a person's quality of life. People can go into debt from a very young age, buying things that they think they want, only to realize what they wanted didn't really bring them much happiness at all.

Discovering what you really want is potentially one of the hardest endeavours you can decide to take on, but it can also have the greatest payoff. If you know what you want, you can paint a vision of what you would like your future to look like. If you can clearly communicate this vision to others, you can solicit help and start turning your vision into reality.

Tip #2 - Think Big

My friend and mentor, John Seminerio, is the founder of many successful ventures. In 2001 he closed the largest seed investment round in Canadian history at $24 million. Previously, as President and CEO of Abatis, he successfully executed a $1.3 billion purchase of his company. John thinks big, he always has, and he does so for good reason.

John once told me that it takes just as much effort to run a convenience store as it does to run a multi-million dollar company. The primary difference is the expected value of the payoff. If you're going to put everything you've got into solving an entrepreneurial problem, why not focus on something that has a big payoff at the end? That's thinking big.

Remember that the payoff doesn't necessarily need to be financial, it just has to be extremely valuable and rewarding to you personally.

Another way to think big about any set of opportunities is to compare the best-case and worst-case scenarios for each opportunity. For example, assume you have decided to start a convenience store. In the worst-case scenario, you fail miserably and you will lose money and time. You'll also have to bankrupt your business and start over. Now consider starting a multi-million dollar company. What's the worst-case scenario? If you fail at developing a potential multi-million dollar business you will lose money, time, and have to bankrupt your business and start over as well.

The downside risk in both scenarios is exactly the same; the worst thing that can happen is that the business goes bankrupt and you have to do something else. Now let's look at the best-case scenario for each business. If you build up the convenience store and have an amazing year, perhaps you will bank a few hundred thousand dollars with the prospect of making a little more money next year. If you build up the multi-million dollar business, you have the potential to sell it, make millions of dollars, and move on to an even bigger project.

If the downside risk is the same, then the laws of expected value suggest that we should focus on those opportunities with the greatest upside. John did this when he set out to build a new supercomputer platform. I'd suggest you do the same when evaluating your entrepreneurial options.

Tip #3 - Focus on Creating Value for Others

Too many entrepreneurs stall their businesses because they focus on how they are going to make money before they focus on how they are going to create value for their customers. My number one priority when starting a business is to have exceptionally happy customers. At HiretheWorld we want every customer to enjoy their experience. If they enjoy their experience they will be back later and use the site again. If they love the site they will tell their friends about us. That brings even more customers. To this day, HiretheWorld relies on referrals from happy customers for about 60% of its business. Keeping customers happy leads to increased business that often leads directly to profits. Entrepreneurs realize that creating value for their customers is the best way to be successful.

HiretheWorld made sure its customers remained happy by presenting them with an exceptional value proposition. In general, you can think of the value proposition in the following way:

Value = Perceived Customer Benefit - Actual Cost of Delivery

The term "perceived customer benefit" is important here. Perception is a powerful tool in business. It is the reason why someone who buys a $400 pair of jeans at 50% off thinks they got a great deal, when in fact the jeans cost only $20 to create. The perceived value can be great even when the actual benefit is not that large.

In HiretheWorld's case, our primary competitors were traditional graphic design companies. If you wanted a logo for your business from our competitors, you would pay them $1000 or more and go through the traditional process.

First, the competitors would collect your information, mock up some suggested logos, collect your feedback, and deliver a finalized product. I first went through this process when I needed a logo for a condominium development and was charged $5000 for it.

At HiretheWorld, we changed the traditional process. The customer would begin by filling in a design brief on the website, paying about $300. This brief then went out to thousands of designers all over the world who were available seven days a week and twenty-four hours a day. The designers then submitted their logo ideas to the website. Each design brief could receive hundreds of designer submissions. The customer would receive hundreds of logo suggestions, but would only have to pay for the one he liked after several rounds of feedback. HiretheWorld provided more design choices, faster, and more conveniently than our competitors. This created an improved value proposition for the customers. By focusing on creating a better value proposition, new customers started flooding in and existing customers started telling their friends.

With success came new ideas. We tried to figure out how to generate more income using a similar model for services other than graphic design. The company worked hard for over a year, adding new services like translation and data entry.

With the growth in offerings our site became much more complicated, to the point where some people didn't think we even did graphic design anymore. Although revenue was going up, design income was dropping and so were our margins. What we didn't account for was how our increase in services would affect the value proposition for our existing customers and our community of designers. As we continued to generalize and offer more choice, our value proposition began to fall when measured against more specialized competitors. Our profits began to shrink, and we started getting negative feedback for the first time in company history.

One particularly difficult day, we had a customer call in that had a Spanish translation done incorrectly. We had no idea what to do about it because no one in our office was fluent in Spanish. In our search for growth, we had sacrificed our customer's happiness and settled on a less than perfect customer experience. This made retaining customers and attracting new ones much more difficult. Our rate of growth slowed and our margins decreased. After almost a year of development, we made the difficult decision to return to a policy of 100% customer satisfaction. This meant abandoning almost a year's worth of code and shutting down many of our new services. It was a tough decision at the time, but we completed the changes and returned to profitability and record growth. Understanding the value proposition from your customer's perspective is a key to entrepreneurial success.

Tip #4 - New Business Ideas are Theories Waiting to be Tested

People often make the mistake of taking their idea for a new business too seriously. They come up with the idea, they work on it, and eventually they become emotionally attached to it. They keep it secret for long periods of time to ensure no one steals it from them. More often than not, this is a dangerous way to think about your business. If you take your initial idea too seriously, you are likely to over invest in it, making you less responsive to potential changes that might improve the design and delivery of your product or service.

Successful entrepreneurs realize that a start-up or new idea is simply a business hypothesis, a theory that suggests how a product or service might deliver value to customers. Since your idea is just a theory, it is your job to test to see if the theory makes sense. You will need to reconsider all the assumptions you made when formulating your idea. Testing these assumptions is the only way to be certain you have designed something valuable to customers. This process is often called "market validation." A business idea without some market validation is often considered worthless, whereas a business idea with positive customer feedback can be quite valuable.

As an entrepreneur, it is your job to figure out the fastest and cheapest way to test your assumptions and move the business forward with confidence. While luck plays a role in any business, luck is usually linked to achieving a positive outcome that you didn't know was going to happen. Entrepreneurs try to take uncertainty out of the equation. If you can be confident in your assumptions, then you know what is going to happen. If you know what is going to happen, then there is no luck, less ambiguity, and little risk.

At HiretheWorld we wanted to build a crowdsourced logo design marketplace. We decided the cheapest way to test our idea was to build a simple prototype.

It took 120 days and $274 to go through this process. By the end of this initial prototype, we had what we thought was a repeatable and scalable business model. We presented our product to potential customers and were able to sell a couple of logos. Over time, we collected enough data and generated enough revenue that we could start approaching potential investors.

Hypothesis testing is a core part of the innovation process and should be embraced by your company, even well after your start-up phase. Employees and customers should be encouraged on a regular basis to generate new ideas to improve your business. Mini experiments can be conducted to see if the ideas were valid. This could be as simple as changing the color of your company's signage or trying a new marketing channel.

The internet has made market validation a much easier experience for entrepreneurs. Data can be easily collected and analyzed. Have a new idea for a business? Why not try LaunchRock.com? It's a website where you can create a landing page in a matter of minutes and begin driving traffic there. Ian Kent, President of NOMAD Micro Homes, designed a house that you can essentially build yourself. He was going to spend $50,000 of his own money to build a prototype that he could market to customers, but he still wasn't sure if anyone would buy it. Instead, he put the design on LaunchRock.com and marketed the home on Craigslist. In a matter of weeks he had over six hundred potential customers in his database and didn't have to spend a dime. With this validation he was comfortable working to move the business forward, and was able to start soliciting the help of potential employees and investors as well. Entrepreneurs find ways to test their new ideas. Don't be afraid to try your new ideas and listen to the suggestions that customers are making.

Tip #5 - Embrace Failure as an Investment in Learning

As an entrepreneur you have to get over the fear of failure. I've personally had to fight with this my whole life. I often find myself evaluating the possible outcomes and overestimating the cost of failure when I'm thinking about taking on a new project or opportunity. It's human nature to be risk averse, but fear generally leads to poor decision making. My biggest regrets in life aren't centered on my failed attempts at new ideas, but rather on the projects that I decided not to take on in the first place.

The fact that a majority of businesses fail should be an empowering force for all entrepreneurs. Every successful entrepreneur has a story about how they failed at something, but once they are successful, no one really cares. In fact, most people would admire them for even making an attempt in the first place. Our entire western economic system is designed to support and embrace failure as a Darwinian process of continuous improvement. Your worst-case scenario in business is always the same: close the doors, take your bumps, and move on to the next one. If you think about it, creating a great business is similar to becoming a great ice skater. You will surely slip and fall at some point during practice or warm-up. Maybe it hurts a little, but nobody really cares that you fell in practice when you have a great routine in competition. To create a great performance, you have to get back up, make some adjustments, and get better. Eventually, you'll be sailing across the ice with the greatest of ease.

When I was in university I applied the same thinking to my scholarship applications. Nobody cared how many scholarships I applied for, people only noticed how many scholarships I won. So, I applied for every single scholarship I could get my hands on. In total I generated over $100,000 in scholarships and awards while at university, and no one ever cared that I failed to receive the million dollars that I actually applied for.

Embrace failure. Befriend it. It will help you accomplish things that you never thought possible.

Tip #6 - Don't Put People on Pedestals

As a businessman and as a politician I have had a reasonable amount of experience with the media. In our oversaturated media culture it is so easy to develop a bias in how we interact with people and situations. The media does a sensational job of either raising individuals up onto pedestals or, more often, knocking them off of one. It's your job to read between the lines and to never buy into the hype. You will do yourself no favours by comparing your "behind the scenes moments" with another person's edited "highlight reel."

Every person in this world is more approachable and more relatable to you than you think. I've met celebrities, professional athletes, prime ministers, presidents, millionaires, and billionaires, and all of them are just like you. So don't be intimidated. If you need to arrange a meeting with the CEO of a Fortune 500 company, then get on the phone, work your networks, and get that meeting. You'll be surprised by how many will eventually pick up your call.

In addition, recognize that true genius is an exceptionally rare trait. The difference between most normal people and exceptionally successful people is a combination of perseverance, effort, and luck. Don't put yourself at a disadvantage by discounting your own capabilities. Start from a position of strength and force everyone else to prove you wrong.

Tip #7 - Get in Front of Real Customers as Fast as Possible and Stay in Front of Them

The faster you get in front of real customers, the better your business will be. Remember that a start-up is not a miniature version of a large company; it is a hypothesis for a potential business. The problem with business hypotheses is that a large majority of them are built on false assumptions and don't survive first contact with your customer. By getting in front of your customers quickly, you can use their feedback to improve your product and strengthen your company's value proposition.

Once you launch your business, it is even more important to stay in contact with your customers. They can keep you apprised of competitors, help you make improvements, and notify you when something is wrong. At HiretheWorld, the customers were a permanent fixture in our development cycle. They would suggest new ideas and features for the site, they would provide us with feedback on our ideas, and they helped us determine what we would spend our development resources on.

Once we launched a new feature or product, we would draw our customer's attention to it and provide multiple channels for them to reach us. This customer feedback loop included a help line, an online helpdesk, and customer support forum. We were never afraid to pick up the phone and call a customer in order to better understand their experience.

There are many exciting new tools you can utilize in order to better track your customer's experience. Online services such as Salesforce allow you to track individual customers at every touch point, no matter who in the company interacts with them. Phone calls, emails, and site usage can all be tracked in a single platform. Zendesk or Desk provide plug-and-play helpdesk support that provides an organized system for dealing with customer questions or complaints. As you answer questions, the responses are automatically recorded online so that many of your future customers can immediately help themselves.

Help communities like Get Satisfaction allow a community of customers to interact with each other. The benefit of having a community is that, in addition to having your customer support answer questions, the community itself is also empowered to answer questions, voice complaints, and propose new ideas. By providing a combination of traditional and online customer support tools, you can ensure that your patrons will always be able to reach you and that you will always have your finger on the pulse of your customer base.

Tip #8 - Take Responsibility, But Don't Take Yourself Too Seriously

Things are going to go wrong. As an entrepreneur it is your job to ensure that things get back on track. There is little time or patience for blame or excuses in the business world. John Wooden, the legendary basketball coach at UCLA with 10 NCAA titles to his credit, often told his players "Losers blame others, winners blame themselves." Blaming someone else for a problem is generally a reactionary measure that may make you feel better in the moment but does nothing to move you closer to achieving your goals. Accept that things will go wrong and be prepared to take ownership of problems regardless of whose fault they might be.

Taking on these responsibilities can be daunting. It's difficult not to take these responsibilities seriously. So it is important to practice Benjamin Zander's Rule Number Six, taken from the sixth chapter of his best-selling book, *The Art of Possibility*. Rule Number Six is simply the idea that you shouldn't take yourself too seriously. Being CEO of a newly founded business can be an ego boosting, then humbling and often lonely exercise. Start-ups can succeed and then quickly fail, and it's easy to become too secure or insecure about your own business acumen, especially when a business is going through rapid growth or hard times.

Often new business owners will consciously or unconsciously place themselves on a management pedestal to maintain a sense of authority. This is particularly true in the face of poor results. This authority is often false and operates through fear. While fear can be an effective short-term tool in an organization, an entrepreneur is ten times better off building an organization based on love and trust rather than fear and loathing. If you build relationships with your employees they are more likely to enjoy their jobs and be loyal to you and the organization. Trusting relationships facilitate an atmosphere of respect and open communication. This means your employees are likely to tell you when something is going wrong and, more importantly, are willing to commit to the effort to try to fix the issue.

At HiretheWorld I'd often proudly introduce myself as the CEO and the janitor. This was because I was always the person responsible for cleaning up messes in the organization. This could mean meeting with a client who was unhappy, or with an investor who didn't close their deal on time. If the staff needed coffee I would make it for them, and if the boardroom was messy after a meeting I would clean it up.

Obviously, there were some jobs that were more important than others, but I wanted everyone in the organization to know that every job, no matter how small, was essential for the success of the company. Tim Ames, a self-described Mr. Fix-it for struggling companies, refers to this mentality as operating with L.O.V.E., or Leaders Offering Value Everyday. In return, our staff was one of the most loyal in the competitive Vancouver tech scene. We hired thirty-two employees over a two-and-a-half year period before we lost our first to a competitive job offer.

Tip #9 - Accept That Effort Does Not Equal Results

Unfortunately the world isn't fair. Equal levels of effort and work don't lead to similar outcomes. Some of this is based on experience, some of this is based on circumstance, but sometimes a lot of it is determined by luck. If your company is out to solve a really difficult problem it might just happen that you will discover the perfect solution on your first attempt, but it might also take 173 attempts. While the first outcome is obviously highly desirable, it is not necessarily a measure of entrepreneurial success. Companies are complex organisms, and no matter how much we try to simplify their DNA, no two companies are ever the same.

For this reason, I highly recommend that you make time to celebrate small wins and try not to beat yourself up too much over temporary problems. This is something that I am personally horrible at. No matter how much success I have, I am always focused on the next goal or the next milestone. While this is sometimes good for business, it's not necessarily always good for your life or that of your employees. Identify the company's priorities, both short-term and long-term, and take the time to enjoy your successes. There will always be a higher mountain to climb, or a slightly higher sales target to hit. Enjoying the journey along the way will ensure that everyone is excited about the next adventure.

Finally, you should recognize that start-ups follow a familiar results trajectory that was first identified in Seth Godin's book *The Dip*. In general, businesses tend to get a lot of early wins and establish a lot of momentum in the first year of operation. You might get a product to the market and even to a few customers. You get a brand new logo and a shiny set of business cards to pass around. You get a lot of positive reinforcement from your friends and a lot of congratulations and offers of support. Soon, however, initial momentum slows as the company exhausts its low hanging fruit and struggles to find a reliable and profitable customer base.

At this point, the entrepreneur invests a lot of resources testing a series of marketing experiments to try to grow its customer base. Since many of these experiments fail, there tends to be a lot of effort without any directly measurable positive results. Seth Godin refers to this part of the start-up cycle as the dip. In the timeline of an organization there tends to be two good "quit points" for an entrepreneur to consider, either prior to entering the dip, or after successfully finding your way out of one. With practice, most businesses can identify where the dip will be in their organization prior to entering it. It's usually the part of the company that is the great unknown, the part that is estimated in the business plan, the part where we can only learn by doing. In most modern start-ups, the dip is associated with market risk or, to put it another way, not knowing enough about the real needs of your customer base.

Be prepared and go into the dip with a plan. Be realistic about your potential success rate, and have your team prepared to fight and claw your way out of it. Estimate how valuable the prize will be, and be prepared to invest the proper level of time and resources to figure a way out. If you can't get out in a way that captures positive value in the long run, then move on. Don't waste further time or money. It might not be fair, but it is the truth and a good entrepreneur should be willing to accept the truth.

Tip #10 - Set a Vision and Build a Road Map

Business plans are overrated. There is a joke among people who raise money that business plans are documents that investors make you write but will never read. The reason that many entrepreneurs are encouraged to write business plans is because it is much cheaper, in both time and money, to investigate a business on paper and abandon it than it is to actually try to build a business and have it fail. On the other hand, most investors don't necessarily trust a fully written business plan because it naturally contains a large number of assumptions that eventually turn out to be false. Luckily, there have been several alternative methodologies which have become popular over the last number of years which can help you avoid writing a full business plan while still examining the business model on paper.

If you have a business idea I would highly recommend you try filling out a business model canvas or a lean canvas. The business model canvas was first developed by Alexander Osterwalder as a tool to help organizations conduct structured analysis on new or existing organizations. It forces you to think through nine fundamental categories of business strategy that every business hypothesis faces, and to organize this information on a single page. The lean canvas I prefer to use was refined by Ash Maurya. Ash's model is better suited to entrepreneurs and start-ups whereas Osterwalder's model is more useful in larger, more established organizations.

The lean canvas is designed to help entrepreneurs construct their business model in ambiguous conditions. By completing a lean canvas it becomes obvious which parts of your strategy is the most uncertain or risky, and therefore requires more action or validation. In addition, the model removes some of Osterwalder's original segments that are less important to start-ups while adding in more relevant criteria. For more information on how to fill in your own lean canvas I highly recommend *Running Lean* by Ash Maurya. You can also easily find a template canvas to fill in yourself by quickly searching the subject in Google.

A lean canvas will help you get the essential information on the table and help propel you into action. The primary problem with business plans is that they fall apart as soon as a single assumption is proven invalid. Suddenly, your beautifully formatted forty page plan is no longer of any use and needs to be redone. By reducing your workload to a one page plan, you can get in front of your customers faster and begin taking actions that will move your business forward. As you begin to execute your business, the drafting of an investment document becomes more of a documentation process than a creative process. This method is more accurate, saves time, and gives you the flexibility to quickly adapt your model as business assumptions change to business facts.

The canvas document can also double as a great tool for pitching future employees and partners on your vision and exactly how you see your business working. You can also put this document in front of your mentors to get feedback and establish relationships early on in the lifecycle of your business. As you identify potential problems and opportunities, you can set actionable goals that determine the next set of priorities for your company. These priorities become the milestones which can then be used to guide the people in your organization, as well as help to identify future resource and funding requirements.

Clearly articulating your vision and business problems will be a critical success factor for your business. Entrepreneurs who can clearly paint a future picture of the business are better able to retain help and delegate responsibility across many individuals. Poor communicators with unclear plans tend to get stuck micromanaging their employees and becoming a bottleneck in their own organization. Imagine your business was a skyscraper. It is almost impossible for you to build such a complex building by yourself, but it's even more difficult to construct such a building if there are no architectural blueprints to follow. Could you imagine how long it would take to complete a building if the owner of the project had to personally tell every contractor where the walls and pipes should be? As an entrepreneur, it's your job to set out your vision and to find a way to communicate it to all of your key stakeholders. By doing this, you empower everyone to help you build your business without necessarily having to discuss every detail with you personally.

The way we handled this communication at HiretheWorld was to implement a series of protocols ensuring that management always had their finger on the pulse of the organization. When our business was just three people, we could easily get away with simply discussing the business priorities on a regular basis. As the organization grew to over twenty full time employees, this methodology became unmanageable. Instead, we would set out ninety day stretch targets every quarter, and hold a management meeting every two weeks where we would discuss our core deliverables. These deliverables would then be presented to the entire team and discussed. Once the team had agreed on an achievable set of targets, we distributed the work and followed our progress on a whiteboard that hung in the office.

Every morning at 10am the whole team would meet for a morning scrum around the whiteboard for fifteen minutes. We would start by reviewing the company's core metrics, including revenue, conversion rate, and site traffic. Every team member also delivered one piece of good news, went over their core achievements from the previous day, and was given an opportunity to raise any challenges that they faced in meeting their goals. If there was a development bottleneck that was preventing you from achieving your targets then this was a forum to bring it up. This process made the entire organization transparent in that everyone knew what everyone else was doing and how their project fit into the goals of the organization. Everyone was aware of the status of each project and its probability of completion. Individuals who were ahead of target were able to divert some of their resources towards projects which were falling behind, and everyone was able to determine early on whether we would require overtime in any given week. For asynchronous team communication we utilized Yammer, a free online internal social network. The benefit of services like Yammer or HipChat is that it keeps the entire team in the loop without interrupting their work flow. You could easily sign-in during a coffee break and check on what all of the other departments in the organization were doing. If you'd like further information on setting up your own operating system, I'd highly recommend reading *Mastering the Rockefeller Habits* by Verne Harnish; it was his map that we followed when building our own management system.

The Bottom Line

There are many benefits to thinking and acting like an entrepreneur. Don't focus on all the reasons you can't be an entrepreneur, instead, focus on all the way you can start being entrepreneurial right now. If the ten tips in this chapter get you excited to continue on, then I encourage you to read the next chapter which covers WHERE to find the people and the money you'll need to get started.

Ten Lessons to Help Get
the People and the Money You Need ⟶ ⟡

This chapter is written to walk you through the process of how I turned a $333.33 loan into a company called HiretheWorld.com. In this chapter we will step through ten lessons learned which follow the story of HiretheWorld in a roughly chronological order. We will start with the day that the company was founded and work through to the point where we hired our first employee. It is my hope that you will find further inspiration in the story as well as identify a number of tools and opportunities that you can use to start your own business.

Sometimes the decision to be an entrepreneur is as difficult as the business itself.

Late one night at Oxford University in the UK, I was passing the time watching random videos on TED.com in my dorm room. I came across a particularly brilliant video by Joachim de Posada who talked about the Stanford Marshmallow Experiments[2]. At the time, I was having an internal debate about whether to start a business or take a stable job after completing my MBA. I credit this video with finally convincing me to stay the entrepreneurial course.

The experiment detailed in the video was focused on the correlation between an individual's ability to delay immediate gratification and the potential or probability of achieving a greater quality of life later on. The experiment was quite simple; a child was seated in a room with a marshmallow placed in front of them. The child was told that the researcher was going to leave the

---

[2] Joachim de Posada. (2009). Don't Eat the Marshmallow!. Available: http://www.ted.com/talks/joachim_de_posada_says_don_t_eat_the_marshmallow_yet.html. Last accessed 20th Oct 2013.

room for a number of minutes and that the child was welcome to eat the marshmallow during that time. However, if the child was able to refrain from eating the marshmallow until the researcher returned, then the child would be given an additional marshmallow as a reward. The experiment went as expected. Some children ate the marshmallow immediately, some became quite anxious waiting for the researcher to come back, and some had no problem whatsoever waiting for their second marshmallow.

The profound part of the experiment came almost twenty years later, when they followed up with the individual test subjects. It turned out that the children who didn't eat the marshmallow had significantly better lives based on a wide variety of measurements. In fact, it turned out to be one of the most statistically relevant determinants of future success that had ever been discovered.

Whether it was true or not, I convinced myself that taking a stable, high paying job after my MBA was equivalent to eating the marshmallow. I decided that I was willing to sacrifice a stable income in order to pursue entrepreneurship and the potential of achieving greater personal rewards in the future. I would start my own business, even if it meant that I had to run it out of my dorm room. It was hard at first, especially after I graduated and headed back home with no real source of income. I left Vancouver with a BMW and a bank account and returned with a 1993 Pontiac Grand Am and considerable debt. Fortunately, I had just spent a year studying venture capital and entrepreneurship, and I knew that there were lots of ways to acquire the resources that I would need.

Lesson #1 - Conditions Will Never be Perfect, Learn to Work With the Resources You Have

In early 2009, I hardly looked like I was in any position to be thinking about starting a business. The stock market crash in the fall of 2008 had come at the worst possible time, striking approximately two weeks prior to having to pay my tuition to attend Oxford. The pound sterling was trading at record highs and I had prematurely quit my job almost a month prior. I felt like the whole financial world was plotting against me. I begrudgingly approached my bank for an emergency line of credit and began my studies at Oxford with over $50,000 in personal debt.

I had planned to focus my studies within the areas of entrepreneurship and finance, but wondered how entrepreneurial I could possibly afford to be when every cup of coffee was being financed with the bank's money. The debt weighed heavily on me and cast a shadow over every purchase I made, no matter how small. I regularly contemplated abandoning the entrepreneurial dream, at least temporarily, until I could get my own finances back in order.

It was early 2009 when I first heard of Professor Stevenson's definition of entrepreneurship which I mentioned in the first chapter:

> *"Entrepreneurship is the pursuit of opportunity without regard for resources currently controlled."*

I was enthralled by the definition. I certainly didn't have very many resources under my control, but I was inspired and decided that if an appropriate opportunity presented itself, I would try to pursue it. This was easier said than done. At Oxford, I was regularly presented with many potentially high paying jobs, and I certainly didn't have any entrepreneurial opportunities to pursue at the time. My motivation regularly flip-flopped. At the time, I kept my options and my mind open to either path. I wrote pro and con lists, I applied for jobs just in case, and I pursued every entrepreneurship related opportunity I could find.

I joined a competitive venture capital team that evaluated entrepreneurial deals against students from other schools. I attended Oxford's Venture Fund competition. When Biz Stone (co-founder of Twitter) or Chris Sacca (a well-known venture investor) came to campus I was sitting in the front row. I wrote a business plan for Twinbro, a non-profit that I had started with my brother, and I put it in front of venture investors to get their opinion. I engaged in endless conversations with fellow students about their ideas, and I even co-founded an entrepreneurial consultancy so that I could work directly with entrepreneurs. I had no idea what was going to come from all of this effort, but I continued to focus just on being involved and trying to create value for other people. I hoped that something good would come out of it, but I had no guarantees.

Every entrepreneur I met had their own tale of hardship. Even the really successful ones, who were now multi-millionaires, all had their own stories of how they had to go through really hard times before they created their "overnight" success story. When Chris Sacca shared that he found himself over $2 million in debt at one point, I questioned if I had what it took to make a similar sacrifice.

My venture capital team was lucky enough to win the European championships. This got our team a free plane ticket to the World Championships in North Carolina. I strategically got a ticket with a layover in Vancouver so that I could visit my girlfriend, and visit a new venture fund that was being started by a previous acquaintance of mine. The founder of the fund was a man that I had a lot of admiration and respect for. I thought it might result in a potential career opportunity if I happened to mention that I was stopping by on my way to "the World Championships of Venture Capital." At this point it still appeared I might be going down the traditional job route after all. I thought that this actually might work out for the best, as working for a venture capital firm would give me the opportunity to work with many entrepreneurs across many businesses.

The meeting at the venture capital firm went nothing like I had expected. The general partner and I talked for over an hour, discussing what I was truly passionate about. We talked about entrepreneurship, politics, and investment. I told him about different options I was considering and he was very open about the personal dilemmas I was facing. He was incredibly empathic and thoughtful in his guidance and his advice. He had previously envisioned himself as a venture capitalist, but had taken almost a twenty year detour because the right career options had always seemed to present themselves. He suggested that I take the proper time to reflect and figure out what I really wanted to do before making any hasty decisions.

As I was exiting his office, I noticed that his logo had changed since I had booked the meeting with him. He said that he got the logo from a new website that crowdsourced graphic design. "What is crowdsourcing?" I asked. He opened a laptop and took me to a site where you could run a contest to get a logo produced. An entrepreneur would describe the company, and hundreds of designers would compete to provide the design, but you would only pay for the one design that you loved. I fell in love with the idea immediately, and did some research to see how competitive the market was. The space was relatively nascent at the time, and having previously spent a lot of money on graphic design, I felt that this business model would have a chance to disrupt the multi-billion dollar graphic design industry. At this point something clicked inside of me and I decided to pursue this opportunity instead of seeking out a job.

Over the course of the next seven days, I sketched out a document that outlined the basic features of a service that would eventually become HiretheWorld. com. Upon returning to Oxford, I put together a basic pitch and ran the idea by my venture capital team. Over Skype, I went through the idea with my brother, Doug, who immediately recognized the company's potential. We agreed to work together but realized that we would need to find someone technical to help us. We began meeting once a week via Skype in order to try to move the business forward as quickly as possible.

Lesson #2 - You Can Start Being an Entrepreneur Part Time

Even though I was excited by the idea of my venture, I still wasn't sure if it was worth putting all of my eggs in one basket. I was still attending my MBA classes full time and had recently landed a great summer gig at Hamilton Bradshaw, a private equity firm run by James Caan, a celebrity in the UK best known for being on Dragon's Den. My brother was simultaneously working on Twinbro and had a high paying job with a helicopter logging outfit. We were continuing to look for a technical partner, but were really only dedicating our evenings and weekends to the venture.

We all knew that a part-time commitment wouldn't work in the long run, but for the present time we could only work with the resources we had available. We agreed to a number of goals and milestones for each of us to hit with hard deadlines. This would ensure that the business moved forward despite our many distractions. As we progressed we were careful to revaluate the time commitments that the opportunity deserved. There are countless businesses with great potential that languish in a perpetual state of half-heartedness and we didn't want to be one of them.

Lesson #3 - Cash and Equity are Two Currencies for the Entrepreneur

In about six weeks we were introduced to Arash Afrooze, a talented coder with the Government of Canada. He had come highly recommended, and Doug and I hoped to get him excited about the idea so that he would be willing to work on it as a side project for a reduced rate. We introduced ourselves online, and I proceeded to pitch him on the idea in the same way that I pitched Doug. Since cash was really tight, we were hoping to compensate him by giving him an ownership stake in the business.

Our initial offer was to cover all of the start up costs of the business and to give him a 10% share of the company. By holding 10% of the company, Arash would be entitled to 10% of all future residual-free-cash-flows produced by the company. It was a way of structuring the deal so that we could delay paying out cash now by promising the potential of substantially more in the future. Another benefit of structuring the deal this way was that Arash would only be rewarded if the company was successful, thus ensuring that his motivation was in line with our own.

Entrepreneurs should be cautious when distributing equity. Equity refers to the ownership stake that someone holds in a business. In the beginning equity seems relatively cheap. Cash is usually in short supply and the company still holds a lot of risk. As the company becomes more successful, the value of the company will begin to outpace the value of cash on hand. Equity distributed undeservedly can be one of the most expensive mistakes an entrepreneur can make.

Lesson #4 - Starting a Company Doesn't Have to be Expensive

Arash's response to our initial offer was swift. "Exactly what expenses are you planning to cover? Hosting and serving costs are basically nothing. If I join I want to be a full partner." Arash was right, there were really no financial costs to start this business, in fact we would be able to develop the site and get our first paying customer while managing to spend only $274 in our first 120 days of operating.

The final structure of the original partnership agreement went something like this. Each founder would put in $333.33 in exchange for 33.3% of the company. We would draw on this initial $1000 in order to cover any expenses we would face. As a partnership, we only required a partnership agreement to get started, which ended up being a one-page document written out in order to appease our bank when we opened up an account. Our first bank account was a no-fee small business account at a local credit union, strategically selected so that we didn't have to pay any fees. The $5 mandatory membership fee is included in the $274 that I mentioned previously.

With the agreement in place we moved quickly to start the business. Our initial plan was simple. Doug and I would continue to work on the functional design and launch strategy for the website, while Arash would create a working prototype that Doug could get in front of prospective customers. We hashed out a formal ninety day plan, a technique I had learned from watching James Caan manage his portfolio investments over the summer. The ninety day plan listed a number of agreed upon milestones, the most important of which was to generate at least a dollar of revenue as quickly as possible.

I had spent some time at a global venture competition at Oxford and noticed that a lot of pre-revenue companies were attracting large amounts of investment in order to test out their start-up hypotheses. I felt that if we could start generating revenue within the company as quickly as possible, that we could either improve our chances of attaining a significant investment or put off the requirement to raise funds altogether.

Although we had all agreed to commit up to $5,000 each to the company, we hoped that we would not have to put in more cash. Our thinking was that we would continue to contribute "sweat equity" to the business and try to either grow revenue organically or seek out an investment. With this in mind, I began putting together a formal investment package for HiretheWorld by documenting all the progress we had made to date. In addition, we set out to identify potential sources of revenue or investment.

Lesson #5 - You Don't Have to Come Up With All of the Money Yourself

Looking back, it is safe to say that HiretheWorld was very thorough in seeking out sources of capital to stay afloat. The founders' initial investment was split between time and money. Arash and Doug committed to a certain number of hours of work per week in order to move the company forward and contributed their $333.33 from their personal savings. I made a similar commitment in time, and financed my $333.33 from my student line of credit. The company was already utilizing savings, sweat equity, and debt to move the company forward. Banks rarely contribute a significant amount of capital to start-up enterprises as their tolerance for risk is much lower than other investors. If a start-up entrepreneur is using debt to finance their business, it is usually personally guaranteed or backed up with significant collateral. Banks usually don't begin to finance companies without security until there is a healthy and reliable revenue stream already being produced.

Since we were unwilling to personally secure a loan and since we were hoping to not have to dip further into our own personal accounts, we did a broad search for alternative sources of capital. The potential sources we identified are detailed below, along with some comments regarding the pros and cons of pursuing each source.

Revenue: By getting customers in the door as quickly as possible, we would be able to start paying our operating costs and potentially invest in further infrastructure and employees. Ideally we would generate enough revenue so that we would never require an investment and remain in complete control of our enterprise. Growing this way would mean growing much slower, as we would have a significantly lower marketing budget and an inability to immediately pay for employees to work on the business full time.

Friends and Family: As HiretheWorld started to grow, a number of friends and family began to get really excited about the potential of the business. There was definitely the possibility that we could receive some form of investment or loan from our friends and family. While these individuals tended to be easier to approach than professional investors, they also brought less value-adding knowledge to the company. In addition, I was adamant that any friend or family member would have to be willing to acknowledge that there was a 90% chance that the company would fail and that they would never get their money back, prior to us accepting any investment from them.

Angel Investors or Venture Capital: Unlike banks, higher risk investors are interested in high growth companies, despite their high failure rate. They invest in a portfolio of many companies, hoping the gains from a home run investment will more than cover the losses from any failures. Attracting investment from these players usually brings significant amounts of cash into a business, but requires a forfeiture of a portion of the ownership and, potentially, control of your company.

Entrepreneurship Competitions and Awards: We identified a large number of business competitions and awards that we could qualify for that offered us opportunities for mentorship, PR, and financial rewards. These competitions tended to include a significant amount of constructive feedback from qualified individuals and prospective investors. Not only did you have a chance to attain an influx of cash if you won, they were also great platforms to raise awareness for your start-up. The downside of these competitions is that they sometimes require a significant time commitment that could distract us from our business.

Incubators and Accelerators: These programs provided varying combinations of mentorship, investment, office space, and training. They are designed to help get a business from an idea to market, and generally offer a small amount of space and money in exchange for some equity.

Government Grants and Tax Credits: We identified a wide variety of government programs that could help subsidize our research and development costs and other human capital costs. We also identified a series of tax credits that could make our company more enticing to potential investors. Government programs that aid start-ups can be a significant source of capital, but they are usually very strict and have time-consuming application processes. If you obtain a grant the time investment is generally worth it, just be aware that you will usually face reporting requirements that may extend for many years.

Lesson #6 - Hope for the Best and Plan for the Worst

In September 2009, Doug found HiretheWorld's first customer at an entrepreneurial meet-up he attended. The client was starting a new home care service and required a logo. Since we didn't have the ability to accept payment on the site quite yet, we received the payment in cash and set out to launch our first design contest. Through the web and social media, we had already acquired five hundred designers who were ready and waiting for the first contest to launch on the site.

With a push of a button the contest went live and a notice was sent to our design community. Then we waited. For hours we hoped that someone, somewhere in the world, would submit a design for our first customer. We didn't have to wait long, as the first design was submitted in less than twenty-four hours, allowing us all to breathe a huge sigh of relief. In five days our first client received 159 unique designs from designers in 18 different countries. The client was so happy with their experience that they have continued to refer our service to many new customers over the years.

Having accomplished our goal of generating revenue, I planned to finish up my MBA at Oxford and fly home to join the team. Although I had known Doug my whole life, I was excited to finally meet Arash, who I had only worked with virtually over Skype. I was sitting in Doug's basement suite, which doubled as HiretheWorld's first head office, when Arash pulled up on his motorcycle. The three of us celebrated our success so far and discussed our potential options to grow the business.

We decided that we would cast as broad of a net as possible, pursuing all possible opportunities that we had previously identified. If we failed in achieving funding or support in any given category, we could, at the very least, fall back on revenue to keep the business alive. At the time, Doug and I were willing to commit to the business full time, but Arash had recently purchased a new house and needed a reliable source of income. We agreed that he would continue to work evenings and weekends as we continued to work on seeking out revenue and investment opportunities.

By January 1, 2010, we had generated approximately $13,000 in revenue and were anxious to get our investment proposal in front of investors. We had lined up at least three business competitions that we were planning to compete in, and we had approached a number of local incubation programs to gauge whether our company might be a successful candidate. In total, we planned to approach over thirty angel investors and venture capitalists. Given the intense competition for resources in the start-up community, we were very aware that we could potentially approach all of these organizations and be universally rejected. With this in mind, we organized a financial strategy that was heavily focused on developing good relationships in our sector. We wanted to make sure that everyone who interacted with our company had good things to say about us, independent of whether they chose to invest or not.

Lesson #7 - Relationships Matter

At the start of 2010, we began our fundraising road show. We pitched to five venture capital firms and approximately twenty angel investors. Our first round of pitches was designed to be friendly and introductory. We focused on the amount of money that we thought we needed to raise and what we would use the money for. We tried to stay away from immediately discussing the financing terms we were looking for so that we could extract more beneficial information from our conversations.

This method meant that the investor focused more on the actual business than the terms of the investment. This allowed us to collect immeasurably valuable feedback very early on and gauge what our potential investor's primary concerns would be. When asked about our proposed valuation, or the price that the investor would have to pay to buy into the company, we would simply state that we were currently running the company off of revenue and weren't sure exactly what valuation was warranted. This was one part strategy and one part truth. The fact was that the valuation is determined by the market, and it was actually this conversation that was helping us establish a price range that a potential investor might be comfortable with. After examining comparable investments in early stage companies, and having many conversations, we believed that an aggressive valuation we could achieve might be somewhere in the two million dollar range. This would mean that an investment of $500,000 would essentially purchase 25% of the business.

As we continued pitching the business to investors, we simultaneously applied for the Venture Connection mentorship program at Simon Fraser University. This gave us access to successful entrepreneurs and investors who we could bounce ideas off as we moved through the fundraising process. One entrepreneur/investor in particular, Jim Derbyshire, would prove to be an invaluable asset to the company as we continued to grow. This is also the program that allowed me to meet John Seminerio, the serial entrepreneur and mentor I discussed in the previous chapter.

Next up, we submitted applications to New Ventures BC, a start-up competition that included ten weeks of mentorship and a potential $123,000 prize package, and the Global Oxford Venture Fund Competition, which invested up to $240,000 in its successful applicants. Over the course of the summer we progressed through the workshops, met more mentors and investors, which led to more pitches. The pitches led to more feedback and even more mentors and investors who were ready to help. At the same time, we were starting to get noticed in the local community. We generated press coverage in the news media that generated more revenue which helped us perform better in competitions. It seemed that every action we took helped support another part of the business, and these synergistic relationships were helping us establish some significant momentum. This momentum helped us attract exceptionally talented individuals who were interested in working for the company.

By March of 2010, we had met our initial target of pitching to thirty investors, but had yet to receive an investment. That being said, we had built a significant pool of relationships, and definitely had established a level of credibility in the community. In the middle of the month we achieved several milestones simultaneously. We established a board of advisors made up of experienced investors and entrepreneurs, and we passed through the first round of both the New Ventures BC and Oxford competitions with flying colors. In addition, we had received our first real equity investment. A group of students who had been consulting for the company in the spring asked if they could invest in the business. We initially said no, and followed it up with a very convincing speech about the high risk of failure that exists in a start-up. Despite this, they were very certain that they wanted to contribute, and eventually they became our first friends and family investment.

In April, we continued working our relationships and growing our networks. We established a connection with most of the local media and began actively pushing stories. We gained a new group of mentors by advancing through to the final round of the New Ventures BC Competition, and we also successfully qualified for the finals of the Oxford Venture Competition. We joined various start-up networks and meet-ups, and started getting better access to information from other individuals and companies in our space who were trying to accomplish similar goals. We used our success at the various competitions to leverage meetings for advice with more senior and experienced individuals, and continued to aggressively expand our presence in the local tech community.

Lesson #8 - Dragon's Den is Not Real Life

Also in April, we applied to be on the hit television series Dragon's Den. Dragon's Den is a popular investment program where entrepreneurs pitch their business to five "Dragon" investors who are prepared to invest in your business on camera if you can impress them. The Canadian group is quite well established, and we were happy to have any of them as investors in HiretheWorld.

Fortunately, Doug and I had a friend who had applied the previous year and filled us in on the details. The application process was fairly simple; you show up in the morning, they give you a time to return, and you give a brief five minute pitch to their executive producers. If they think your company would make good television, then you fly to the studio to record an episode.

We had very little prepared on the final day of applications, but Doug and I went to the tryouts knowing that there would be a delay. Once we were given our time slot, we drove to a McDonalds a couple of blocks away and worked on a pitch. In general, we followed Dave McClures "VC Viagra" pitch format[3], a kind of cheat sheet for companies trying to sell themselves to investors. It took three hours to complete the entire PowerPoint presentation. We spent the next two hours practicing and then made our way back to the tryouts. We pitched the idea of holding a global contest redesigning the Dragon's Den logo as a way of successfully promoting the investment while entertaining a TV audience. The producers loved it and even offered to pay for 50% of the cost of the contest.

Our Dragon's Den appearance was scheduled just three days before we were scheduled to be in Oxford for the final round of the Global Venture Competition. As finalists, Oxford had generously provided our airfare, while Dragon's Den had provided a $750 cash subsidy towards travel. We arranged for a flight that had a twenty-four hour layover in Toronto so that we could film the episode and carry on to Oxford. I posted on my Facebook account that we were going to be in Toronto, and a friend of ours generously offered us his living room to sleep in. Thanks to our entrepreneurial initiative, HiretheWorld ended up turning a "profit" of about $300 on the trip.

When we arrived in the Dragon's studio, we were provided make-up and scheduled to go in front of the Dragons immediately after lunch. They arrived and we were asked to wait on top of some wooden scaffolding that was built above the set. This gave the audience the visual effect that we were walking downstairs, or into a den, when really we were walking into a very well lit, black box.

---

3 Dave McClure. (7th Oct 2009). How to Pitch a VC. Available: http://www.slideshare.net/UTR/how-to-pitch-a-vc-dave-mcclure. Last accessed 20th Oct 2013.

We started our pitch as requested, asking for the $2 million valuation that we had previously determined from speaking with other investors. The Dragons immediately scoffed at the investment and began to describe a number of reasons why the company was either worth less or that their personal investment was worth more. Doug and I specifically went into Dragon's Den with the mission to get a deal. In our minds, a deal at any valuation would guarantee at least eight minutes of national TV coverage, whereas not completing a deal might only get us a single minute or less. We went into negotiations and enjoyed the amusing banter that arose between the individual Dragons. Large segments of time went by where we stood silently listening to the Dragons discuss the potential investment. Offers were made and we eventually sought time in a private booth in the back in order to discuss our options.

Our discussion was pretty straightforward; we knew we needed to get a deal, but felt that we could push back to a get better terms. If push came to shove, we would take a deal and then try to negotiate better terms with another investor during the due diligence period. The due diligence period is the time when an investor and an entrepreneur complete their final research prior to signing off on a deal. In the end, we offered to give up 30% of our business for an investment of $280,000. We shook hands on the deal and then recorded some additional footage so that the Dragons could slip in several witty comments they had been working on over the course of the negotiation. We exited triumphant, extremely excited about getting a deal, as well as landing some national air time and some great investors.

Immediately upon exiting, we were approached by one of the Dragon's assistants who asked us to sign an exclusivity agreement so that we could not approach other investors while we were negotiating with them. We advised that we would pass the document on to our lawyers before we would agree to sign and headed to the pub to celebrate.

It is important to understand that unlike what is seen on TV, a majority of investments on Dragon's Den rarely go through. Deals often fail in due diligence, either because the entrepreneur failed to provide an accurate description of their business or because some other factor caused the deal to be scrapped. During this period, the investor or the entrepreneur can choose to back out of the deal for almost any reason. It is fair to say that the producers of the show are far more interested in entertainment than in ensuring that quality business deals are actually completed. In our case, we hoped to hold the Dragons to their deal, but had no intention of signing the exclusivity document as we wanted to keep our options open.

Lesson #9 - Investors Like to Say No, Fortunately You Only Need One to Say Yes

We proceeded to Oxford and presented our final pitch and business plan. At this point we had drafted over thirty versions of the plan and had pitched the business to over fifty investors and mentors. The constant rejection and iterations paid off, as we were the only team successful in securing an investment at the competition that year. We had received a solid endorsement from the fund's benefactors, UK retail magnate Sir Phillip Green and billionaire investor David Bonderman, and were advised that we would start immediately working through due diligence.

After arriving back in Vancouver and celebrating the victory with Arash, we leveraged the success to beef up our final pitch in the New Ventures BC Competition. We were able to add Oxford to our list of investors, as well as demonstrate our latest growing revenue numbers to the judging panel that consisted of over ten venture capitalists. This was enough to put us over the top and, in early September of 2010, we narrowly won the New Ventures BC competition, beating out over 160 other businesses. This secured an additional $100,000 in non-dilutive cash and $23,000 in prizes. It wasn't until the third pitcher of beer that the team realized that the ceremonial envelope actually had the check for $100,000 inside of it. These back-to-back victories gave the team the confidence we needed to commit to the venture full time and to begin looking for additional full-time employees.

We commenced due diligence with Oxford and began recruiting our first hire, a full-time user interface designer from Simon Fraser University (SFU). We also entered a competition through SFU's Venture Connection incubator program to secure a year's worth of free office space at their technology center. We were successful and were just moving into the brand new office when disaster struck. It turned out that Oxford's investment board had decided they did not want to lead an investment for a company that was not located in the UK. They were still willing to invest, but they wanted us to find a lead investor who was located in North America, and who was also willing to match their investment. This meant we had less than sixty days to find an investor who was willing to write a check for $240,000 or risk losing the entirety of the investment.

Lesson #10 - Everything is Not Going to Go According to Plan, Be Adaptable

Needless to say, the team started to freak out a little. We had over a hundred thousand dollars in the bank, and increasing revenue, but most of us had already started adjusting our lives around the idea that the investment was a sure thing. If we started paying the founders' salaries alongside a new graphic designer, we would have less than a year's worth of cash and would be unable to hire more full-time developers.

Fortunately, through some creativity and a little luck, we were able to find a solution. One of our previous angel groups had expressed significant interest in investing in us but was not certain about our proposed valuation. On the following Monday, I requested a meeting with one of their directors and pitched him our idea. I told him about the deal we got from Oxford. He was very congratulatory, but restated their company's position of not wishing to come in at such a high valuation. Realizing this, I suggested that we could actually utilize a series of resources to essentially get their investment in at half the valuation. The investor was more than intrigued and asked me to describe how this might be possible.

The solution was relatively simple given the information we had learned through our previous research. There was an angel tax credit which this specific investment group would qualify for. The credit essentially guaranteed a return of 30% of their investment if they invested in a qualified Canadian company for any value up to $200,000. This meant that a $240,000 investment would immediately return to them $60,000, resulting in a real investment of $180,000. In addition, I was aware that the investment group was sitting on a large amount of valuable office space in Vancouver's Gastown, an emerging tech center. This office was basically sitting empty despite the group having a three year lease on the property.

I suggested that HiretheWorld would pre-lease two years of space for up to twenty employees at a rate of $20,000 per year, thereby lowering the cash investment by a further $40,000 to $140,000. In addition, since they were going to be responsible for attending board meetings and leading the investment, we would pre-pay a further management fee equivalent to $10,000 per year. The effect of these transactions was that the angel group had a cash outlay of only $120,000 while Oxford had a total outlay of $240,000. Both investors agreed to the deal and on December 24, 2010, HiretheWorld secured its first major round of financing at an adjusted $2.1M valuation.

Our first full-time employee was hired in January 2011, and we funded the first three months of her salary through a government grant designed to promote the hiring of recent graduates. In fact, we would use our initial investment to leverage an additional $400,000 in funding from various grants and tax credits. The investment allowed us to increase the size of our team from three to twenty-four, and we set out to quickly expand the business.

We utilized stock options to heavily incentivize our staff, but also to attract top talent at a discount to market rates. This allowed us to hire more people, and take advantage of more funding programs which often cited employment as an important factor in their eligibility criteria. This series of successful events and growth dramatically increased our profile and press coverage that again led to even more business and revenue.

By the middle of 2011, HiretheWorld had successfully transitioned into its next stage of growth. The founders had successfully turned $333.33 and part-time employment into significant ownership in a successful and growing enterprise. Best of all, each of us were now being paid to come in and build our own business every day. Over time, I paid off my student debt and was able to rebuild my savings account, all while building equity in my business.

In addition to financial security, we had all acquired a set of life skills that were invaluable. We learned to build something from nothing. We had pursued an opportunity without regard for the resources we had currently controlled, and succeeded. We had become seasoned entrepreneurs. It was an empowering experience that opened our eyes to the true potential of the opportunities that existed all around us. It was like a light switch had been flipped, and suddenly nothing was impossible. It was an amazing feeling, an empowering feeling, and was something that I hoped I would be able to share with others.

Closing Thoughts

Since returning from Oxford, I have spent my time pursuing different entrepreneurial ventures as well as teaching the subject at conferences, workshops, and universities. It is a personal passion of mine to arm more people with the tools of the entrepreneur. These individuals can then work to improve the quality of their own lives and the lives of every Canadian.

In 2010, I co-authored a paper entitled *Global Gazelles: A National Strategy for High Growth Entrepreneurship in Canada.* A key finding of our report was that there is a relative scarcity of entrepreneurship education and training in Canada. It is part of the reason why Canada is unique in leading the world in research, but is coming up short in terms of innovation and commercialization.

It is my hope that Canadians will look for opportunities to provide exposure to entrepreneurial experiences through the traditional education system. This includes elementary students as well as high school and university students. I also believe that it is important to share these skills across multiple faculties, and break through the business faculty's usual claim to the discipline. Entrepreneurship includes a number of skill sets useful to all Canadians, not just Canadian business owners.

In addition, I hope that the entrepreneurial stories in this book have inspired you enough to have you consider trying an entrepreneurial project, in your own company or in another. I also hope that the thirty points provided you some additional tools and inspiration to encourage you to get started. I wish you well in your future endeavours, and please feel free to reach out to me in the future, as I love to hear the stories of entrepreneurial Canadians.

To your future success!

Extra Resources: ✺

I recognize that I can't relay everything you need to know about entrepreneurship in three chapters or even in a single book. You can't even relay everything in a single "extra resources" list. I've included the following incomplete list of resources that I've enjoyed and utilized during my entrepreneurial adventures.

Google. Literally the answer to every question. Thank you Google.

- *The Dip* by Seth Godin
- *The 4-Hour Work Week* by Timothy Ferriss
- *The Lean Startup* by Eric Ries
- *Running Lean* by Ash Maurya
- *The Art of Possibility* by Rosamund Stone Zander and Benjamin Zander
- *Mastering the Rockefeller Habits* by Verne Harnish
- *forentrepreneurs.com* by David Skok
- *Crossing the Chasm* by Geoffrey A. Moore
- *Outliers* by Malcolm Gladwell
- Dave McClure's *"How to Pitch a VC"* available here: http://www.slideshare.net/UTR/how-to-pitch-a-vc-dave-mcclure
- Reid Hoffman's *"LinkedIn's Series B Pitch to Greylock"* available here: http://reidhoffman.org/linkedin-pitch-to-greylock/
- *Venture Deals* by Brad Feld
- *The Startup Owner's Manual* by Steve Blank and Bob Dorf
- *Rich Dad, Poor Dad* by Robert Kiyosaki
- *The Four Steps to the Epiphany* by Steve Blank
- *The Art of the Start* by Guy Kawasaki
- *Presenting to Win: The Art of Telling Your Story* by Jerry Weissman
- *Double: How to Double Your Revenue and Profit in 3 Years or Less* by Cameron Herold
- Other resources available at http://terrybeech.com/